THE SILENT SUPERWOMEN

THE INVISIBLE BURDEN OF BEING EVERYTHING TO EVERYONE

PALAK BHANDARI

To my mom and dad —
for your quiet strength, endless support, and the kind of
love that makes everything feel possible.
This book exists because you taught me to listen, to care,
and to never stop speaking up for others.

Contents

PREFACE

The Silent Superwomen was born out of quiet observation—and deep concern.

Everywhere I looked, I saw women carrying invisible burdens. Mothers, students, professionals, daughters, caregivers—each of them juggling countless roles, often with little acknowledgement of the mental and emotional cost. Their strength was undeniable, but so was their silence.

This book is a collection of stories inspired by those women. While some are based on lived experiences and others are shaped by observation and research, each one reflects a larger truth: that many women are struggling quietly, and their mental health deserves more attention, compassion, and support.

My goal is not just to tell their stories, but to invite reflection. If even one reader feels seen, understood, or moved to start a conversation—then this book has served its purpose.

Thank you for taking the time to read it.

I

Healer Who Hurts

The room is quiet, saved for the soft hum of the air conditioner, struggling against the thick, heavy heat of the afternoon. The sunlight spills through the blinds, casting slivers of warmth onto the worn wooden floor, and for a moment, everything feels still, peaceful, and untouched. In this space, there are no expectations, no demands. It is a sacred place—one of safety, a sanctuary where the world outside fades, where people come to heal. The smell of lavender and chamomile lingers in the air, a careful touch to soothe the soul.

Evelyn sits across from me. I know her well by now. She's in her early thirties, with a face that carries the weight of something unspoken, a burden she's carried for years. She leans forward, clasping her hands tightly together, her nails a soft shade of pink, her fingers trembling ever so slightly. Her eyes are red, like the last streaks of daylight before the night comes, but there is a spark there, a quiet strength trying to break through.

She speaks, her voice a soft whisper that seems to tremble at the edges of every word. "I don't know if I can do this anymore. I've tried so hard. I feel like I'm drowning, but everyone keeps telling me to swim."

Her words, like all the others before hers, spill out with the kind of desperate hope that only someone who's lost in the deep can muster. Her pain feels real, raw, and palpable. I nod slowly, letting the silence settle between us. I've heard these words before, the same cry for help dressed in different faces, different names. But every time, it feels just as heavy.

"I hear you, Evelyn," I say gently. "It's okay to feel like that. It's okay to not have all the answers. We don't always have to swim right away. Sometimes, it's just about staying afloat."

She nods, as if these words are an anchor for her—a fleeting moment of understanding. The clock ticks on the wall, each second marked by the steady pulse of time, a reminder that this moment, this breath, is all we truly have. She takes a shaky breath, releasing a long sigh, the weight of her soul heavy in the quiet room.

And yet, as I sit there, listening to her, something stirs deep inside of me.

In the safety of my own office, behind the comfortable chair I sit in, the uniformity of my desk, and the shelves filled with countless books on psychology and wellness, there is a part of me—a part I can never show Evelyn or any of my clients—that aches with a longing that no amount of patient listening, or advice, could ever soothe. I know that she sees me as the calm in the storm, the one who holds the answers. She sees me as someone strong, someone who has it all together.

But the truth is, I don't. I never have.

The morning had begun like any other. I had woken up to the soft sound of the birds chirping outside my window, a normal reminder that the world had been turning while I was asleep. I went through my routine—shower, coffee, breakfast. Simple things. Things that shouldn't take too much thought, shouldn't be so complicated. But even then, the thoughts started to creep in. The empty ones. The ones I always try to push away but always find a way to pull me under.

The truth is, I don't know how I've come to be in this place, this life of helping others while I am quietly crumbling beneath it all. I wonder, sometimes, when it all started. Was it in college, when I first started to study psychology and realized how much I didn't know about myself? Was it during my first internship, when I saw the suffering of people that I felt too small to heal? Or was it when I first sat across from someone—someone just like Evelyn—and thought to myself, I don't even know how to help myself, let alone anyone else?

But I smile. I listen. I hold space.

I hold their hands, their brokenness, their pain. And for them, I am the safe place. For them, I am the healer. But no one ever asks about me. No one ever wonders what happens to the person who listens, who absorbs all that pain and carries it quietly in the depths of their own soul.

The clock ticks again, and Evelyn shifts in her seat, her eyes scanning the room as if searching for the words she can't find. I have seen this before. I've seen it too many times to count—the way people talk about their pain like it's something that can be fixed. Something that can be "cured" if only they could understand it enough, if only they could talk through it enough, if only they could find the right words to make sense of it all.

I know better than anyone that pain is never that easy.

Pain is never something you can just talk away. It doesn't live in words, or in sessions, or in the gentle touch of a hand. Pain lives in the body, in the heart, in the spaces between breaths. It lingers in places where no one can reach, in places where the mind can't bear to go. I know that feeling all too well.

The hum of the air conditioner breaks the stillness again, and Evelyn's voice cuts through the silence once more. "I don't know what's wrong with me. I feel like I'm losing myself. Like I'm becoming someone I don't even recognize."

And that's when it hits me—that feeling. The feeling that gnaws at the edge of every moment in my life, that quiet despair that no one can see. That nagging question: Who am I, really?

I'm a therapist. I'm the one everyone comes to for answers, for peace. I'm the one everyone expects to have it all figured out. I'm the calm in the storm. The rock. The steady presence in the chaos of other people's lives. But no one knows the truth.

I'm just like them. I'm just as lost, just as broken, just as desperate for answers that seem to slip further and further from my grasp every day.

The irony is suffocating. I have the tools, the knowledge, the experience to guide others through the darkest parts of their minds, but I can't seem to find a way to guide myself through mine. I sit across from Evelyn, her voice trembling in my ears, and I want to tell her the truth. I want to say, I understand. I feel it too. But I don't know how to fix it. I don't know how to heal myself.

But I can't. Because in my world, I am the healer. I am the one who has all the answers. I am the one who listens and never breaks. I am the one who fixes.

But the truth is—I am broken, too.

And every day, I wonder if I'll ever be whole again.

The silence stretches between us, thick and heavy, but it is not uncomfortable. It is the kind of silence where two people understand each other without words.

Evelyn looks at me, her eyes searching mine. "I don't know what's wrong with me, but I just... I just need someone to say it's going to be okay."

And in that moment, I realize that I will never be able to say it with the same conviction I say it to others. Not because I don't believe it, but because I can't promise something I don't know is true.

Instead, I just nod and say the only thing I can. "It's okay to feel like this. And it's okay to not have all the answers. We're in this together."

And that, somehow, feels like enough.

For now, anyway.

Evelyn's eyes soften at my words, and for a moment, the tense muscles in her shoulders release. She exhales as though a weight has shifted, even if only a little. It's a small step, but it's enough. I watch her, listening to the change in her breath, the way her eyes flicker with a glimpse of hope. A faint light, the kind that tries to pierce through a fog, even if only momentarily.

But the fog is thick, and I feel it too.

I shift in my seat, trying to hide the tightness that is settling in my chest. The weight of my own unspoken truth is never far behind, never far from the surface. As Evelyn opens up more, telling me about her struggles at work, the strain in her relationship with her partner, the expectations of her family, I can't help but wonder: What happens when the healer runs out of words?

I've asked myself that question countless times before, standing in front of the mirror, fixing my gaze in a way that hides the exhaustion in my eyes. I've looked at the tired woman staring back at me, the one who has been running on fumes for so long that it feels like she's forgotten what it's like to feel whole.

My hands are shaking a little now, but I tuck them under the table, hiding the tremor that betrays the calm exterior I've spent so long perfecting. I wonder, for a brief moment, if Evelyn notices. If she can see through the thin veil of my composure.

But then, she starts to cry. The tears come slowly at first, just a trickle down her cheek, as though she's unsure whether to let it all spill out, afraid of being too vulnerable, too much. But vulnerability, like anything else, builds momentum. It doesn't stay quiet for long.

I see her fight it—the instinct to hold it together, to remain composed. But the dam breaks, and soon she is openly sobbing, her shoulders trembling with the weight of all the things she's held back for so long. The tears fall freely now, and I sit there, in this familiar role, waiting for her to find the words again, waiting for the storm inside her to subside.

And I realize, in that moment, that this is what I do: I hold space. I am here to listen, to bear witness to the chaos that others can't bring themselves to face. I am here to absorb it, to be the one they trust, even if it means leaving pieces of myself behind with each person who enters my office.

As Evelyn weeps, I find myself staring at the floor, my mind racing. The weight of her sorrow, though her own, begins to press against me. It's a familiar sensation, this quiet ache, this sense of carrying another person's pain.

And as I watch her cry, I wonder when the last time was that I let myself fall apart. When was the last time I let myself cry, without fear of judgment, without the need to be strong, to be the one with all the answers?

The truth is, I don't remember.

The session finally draws to a close, and Evelyn wipes her eyes, embarrassed by the flood of emotion she couldn't control. I reassure her gently, telling her that it's okay to cry, to feel it all. But inside, I can't help but wonder why I can't allow myself the same grace. Why I have become so good at hiding the cracks in my own soul.

She stands up, a little steadier now, and I hand her a box of tissues, watching her as she dabs at her eyes. She gives me a faint, tired smile, the kind that says she's still fighting but is at least ready to face another day.

"Thank you," she says quietly, her voice still a little raw. "I didn't know how much I needed to just... let it all out."

"You don't have to thank me," I reply softly. "You've done the hard part. You've taken the first step."

She nods, though there's still a flicker of doubt in her eyes, a hesitation that lingers even as she walks toward the door. I can feel it too, that ever-present sense of uncertainty that hangs in the air. She doesn't believe me, not entirely. She doesn't believe that this small release, these few moments of vulnerability, will change anything. She doesn't yet know that healing doesn't come in perfect packages, that it comes in fragmented moments, like this one.

I watch her leave, the door clicking shut behind her, and for the first time in the session, I allow myself to breathe deeply. My chest feels tight, a little too tight, like something is lodged in there, pressing against my ribs. I glance at the clock on the wall—five minutes to the next appointment.

I lean back in my chair, closing my eyes for a moment, and I let myself feel the weight of the day, the heaviness that has been settling in my bones for weeks now. The truth is, I'm tired. Exhausted, in ways I can't explain. I try to push the thought away, to focus on the next person who will walk through my door. I know I have to be ready for them. I have to be the rock again.

But the truth is, I'm not a rock. I'm not unbreakable. I am soft, fragile, like everyone else. I wonder if I'll ever allow myself the space to fall apart, to stop holding it together for everyone else. I wonder what it would feel like to not be the one who always has to listen, always has to fix. I wonder what it would feel like to be the one who is cared for, for once.

The door opens, and my next client steps in, shaking me from my thoughts. I smile, quickly wiping the tears that I didn't know had started to gather in my eyes. I stand up, pushing the weight of everything down into a corner of my mind, just for a while.

"Hi," I say, my voice calm, steady. "Welcome. Please, take a seat."

They sit down across from me, and I begin the dance again—the one where I listen, where I absorb, where I hold the space. I let their words wash over me, and I do my best to guide them through their pain. I ask the questions that will help them uncover the roots of their suffering. I offer them advice, just as I've always done. But inside, there's a quiet whisper that never goes away: You are just as broken as they are.

The day passes in a blur. Another session, another face, another person to help. Each one walks in, and I become their therapist—the one who listens, who guides. And then they leave, one by one, each of them a little lighter, a little more hopeful, and I am left alone again, with the echo of their pain still lingering in the air.

When the last person leaves, I lock the door behind them, the sound of the key turning in the lock almost deafening in the silence of the office. I stand there for a moment, leaning against the door, my hand on the cool wood, letting the quiet settle around me.

And then, for the first time today, I let myself breathe fully. The weight of the day, the weight of everyone else's pain, settles into my chest. It presses down on me, and I feel the ache again, the quiet sadness that I've been carrying for so long. I close my eyes for a moment, just a moment, and I let myself feel it—every ounce of the exhaustion, every fragment of my own unhealed wounds.

But the thing about pain is that it doesn't have to define us. It doesn't have to break us.

I let out a shaky breath, wiping away a tear that has slipped down my cheek without my permission. It's a small thing, this tear. But it feels like a small victory.

Because for once, I allowed myself to be human.

The air in my office is thick with silence now. The kind of silence that feels like it carries more weight than a thousand words. The kind that lingers after the rush of people has passed, after the world has been poured out in confessions and broken stories, leaving only the soft echo of what was said.

I sit at my desk, looking at the clock on the wall, watching the seconds pass by in their slow, relentless rhythm. The ticking is louder now. In this space, the sound of time feels like a heavy drumbeat, marking each moment as something that passes and is gone. I can almost feel the weight of those moments settling in the pit of my stomach, as though each one of them belongs to me.

But I try not to think about that too much. I'm good at pushing thoughts away, at silencing the noise inside. I've had to be. It's what makes me good at my job. People come to me for answers. For guidance. For solace. And I give it to them, with everything I have. Every ounce of empathy, every ounce of energy, I pour into them. Because I know the value of feeling seen. I know the relief that comes when someone listens, truly listens, and makes space for your pain.

I just don't know how to make space for my own anymore.

I stand up, walking across the room to the small window that overlooks the street. The sun is starting to dip below the horizon, casting a soft amber glow across the city below. The streets are filled with people walking, talking, living, moving through their lives without knowing the weight that I carry, the quiet battle I fight every day.

The city looks so alive, so full of possibility. And yet, in this moment, I feel so far removed from it. I wonder, if I stepped into that world below, would anyone see me? Would anyone notice that I am not as whole as I pretend to be? Would anyone recognize the quiet ache that sits just beneath my skin?

A thought crosses my mind, an unsettling thought. What if I am not actually helping anyone? What if all these hours spent listening to other people's struggles, offering them advice, offering them support—what if it's just a distraction from my own inability to face what's inside of me? What if my whole career, my whole identity, has been built on the facade that I have it all figured out? What if I'm just as lost as everyone else, but I've convinced myself that being the guide means I can't admit that?

I shake my head, pushing the thought away. No, I remind myself, that's not it. I can't afford to think like that. I can't afford to doubt myself now, not when people rely on me. Not when people trust me.

But the doubt lingers.

I return to my desk and open the drawer, pulling out the small leather-bound journal I keep hidden from view. It's not for my clients, not for anyone else. It's for me. Though I've rarely written in it—who has time to reflect when they're so focused on fixing others?—I've come to realize that it's the one place where I can let the mask slip. Even if only for a moment.

I open it to a blank page, the pen feeling foreign in my hand as I hover over the lines, uncertain. But then, slowly, the words begin to spill out:

I don't know how much longer I can do this.

I pause, the pen hovering over the paper as the weight of the words sinks in. It's an admission that I have been avoiding for so long. The truth that I have been holding inside, the one I refuse to acknowledge in front of anyone, least of all myself.

I begin to write again, the words coming faster now:

I don't know how much longer I can keep pretending. Pretending that I'm okay. Pretending that I have it all together. But I am not okay. I haven't been okay for a long time. I keep telling everyone else that it's okay to not be okay, but I don't believe it for myself. I tell my clients that they don't have to have all the answers, but I feel like I should. I feel like I should be able to fix everything, to have the answers, to know what to do. But I don't.

The words flow onto the page, raw and unrefined, like a rush of water breaking through a dam. It's like I've been holding this flood inside for years, and finally, the words are finding their way out. I can't stop them now, and I don't want to.

I am tired. I am so tired. I am so tired of holding it together for everyone else, but who is there to hold me? Who is there to help me when I need it?

I pause again, my fingers trembling. I've never allowed myself to be this vulnerable, this honest. It feels dangerous, like I'm exposing something that shouldn't be seen. But at the same time, there's something deeply freeing about it. Like I'm finally letting go of a burden that has been slowly crushing me.

I need help. But I don't know how to ask for it. I don't even know who I would turn to.

The words echo in my mind, the truth of them reverberating in my chest. It's a truth I have denied for so long. I have always been the one who helps. The one who listens. The one who heals. But when did I stop asking for help? When did I stop giving myself the permission to be human? To be imperfect?

And in that moment, as the ink soaks into the page, something shifts inside me. I can't explain it, but it's as if I've finally allowed myself to breathe. To admit that I'm not okay. To admit that I need more than I have been giving myself. I've been living this lie for so long, thinking that my worth is measured by what I give to others, that I forgot to value what I need for myself.

I look down at the journal, the words staring back at me, and I feel a quiet sense of relief wash over me. It's not the kind of relief that comes from fixing everything. It's the kind that comes from simply acknowledging the truth.

The doorbell rings. I glance at the clock again, startled by how quickly time has passed. Another session. Another person. Another soul to listen to.

I quickly shove the journal back in the drawer, closing it with a soft click. The world outside my office is waiting, and I know I have to be ready. I take a deep breath, pushing the rawness of what I've just written deep inside, tucking it away where it can't be seen. For now, I will be the therapist again. The one with all the answers. The one who listens.

I stand up, smoothing my blouse as I walk to the door, ready to greet my next client with a calm smile. But even as I do, I feel something inside me shift. Something that I can't fully understand, but something that feels like a first step toward something new.

Maybe it's okay to not have all the answers. Maybe it's okay to ask for help. Maybe, just maybe, I can be both the healer and the one who needs healing.

With that thought, I open the door, ready to listen again. But this time, there's a quiet knowing inside me. That this—this quiet battle, this journey—isn't over. And I don't have to face it alone.

The new client steps in, her eyes cautious, her shoulders hunched in that familiar posture that signals someone who is carrying too much weight, but hasn't learned how to put it down yet. She's young—probably in her early twenties—her hands fidgeting with the strap of her bag as though it's the only thing that can anchor her to this moment.

I offer her a soft smile, the one that feels automatic now, the one that is meant to be reassuring but, deep down, feels a little like a mask.

"Hi, I'm Evelyn," she says, her voice small, like she's testing the air to see if it's safe to speak. She doesn't seem to know what to say next, so I fill in the silence, guiding her to the chair across from me.

"It's nice to meet you, Evelyn. Feel free to make yourself comfortable," I say, though I'm not sure how comfortable anyone can really feel in a space like this. It's a place where people come to face their darkness, where vulnerability is allowed to seep out like water through the cracks in a dam.

She hesitates for a moment before sitting down, folding her hands in her lap. She doesn't look at me, not directly—her gaze is fixed on the floor, like she's trying to find the right words, but they're caught somewhere in her throat, stuck behind the walls she's built around herself.

"So, Evelyn, what brings you in today?" I ask, my voice gentle, though inside, I feel a flicker of impatience. It's not her fault, of course. It's just the way I'm wired. I am always ready to dive in, ready to solve, ready to help. But today, there's a slight hesitation, a reluctance that doesn't sit well with me.

Evelyn finally lifts her head, but only enough to meet my eyes for a fleeting second before looking away again. There's a sadness there, an exhaustion that feels like it's been building for years. It's the kind of tiredness that goes beyond physical weariness—it's in her soul. I've seen it before. I know it too well.

"I don't even know," she says, her voice cracking just a little. She takes a shaky breath and looks out the window, as though the answer might be waiting for her out there in the world. "I just... I don't know how to handle everything anymore."

I lean forward slightly, trying to make my presence softer, more inviting. "What do you mean by everything?"

She bites her lip, clearly trying to hold it together, but the dam that has been holding back all her emotions is starting to crack. The words come out in a rush, tumbling over each other, her chest rising and falling with the weight of them.

"I don't know how to do this. How to be… enough. I feel like I'm failing at everything—at work, at my relationships, at being a good daughter, a good friend. And I'm just so tired. So tired of pretending like it's all fine when it's not. But I don't know how to stop pretending."

Her voice shakes with the last words, and before I can stop her, her eyes fill with tears, and she quickly wipes them away, embarrassed by the sudden rush of vulnerability.

But I see her. I see the fragility in her words, the heaviness in her silence, and I know what she's really saying. It's not just about being "enough." It's about the pressure of trying to keep up with everyone's expectations, of wearing a mask every day and pretending to be someone she's not. It's about the exhaustion of carrying the weight of the world, even though she's never asked to bear it.

She's afraid. Afraid of being seen for who she really is—broken, tired, imperfect. And she's afraid of admitting that to anyone, especially herself.

I nod slowly, my heart tightening in empathy. "Evelyn, it's okay to feel like you're not enough. It's okay to feel like you're struggling. You don't have to carry everything alone. And you don't have to pretend that you're fine when you're not. This space is for you to let it all out. You don't have to be perfect here."

She looks at me then, her eyes filled with a mixture of disbelief and relief, as though she can't quite understand how someone could give her permission to let go of the weight she's been carrying.

"But I should be able to handle it," she says softly, the words slipping out almost by accident. "I should be stronger."

I feel a wave of frustration rise within me, but I keep my voice steady, reminding myself that it's not her fault. It's society's fault for making us believe that being strong means doing it all alone, never showing weakness, never admitting that we need help.

"Evelyn," I say, my voice firmer now, "strength is not about carrying everything on your own. Strength is about allowing yourself to feel, to ask for help when you need it, to be honest with yourself about where you are. Strength is about accepting that it's okay to not have all the answers, to not always be okay."

She looks at me again, her eyes searching mine, looking for something—some sign that she's not as broken as she feels.

I don't have all the answers. I don't even have a fraction of them. But I can offer her this moment. I can offer her my presence, my attention, my willingness to listen. That's all I can give her right now.

And, perhaps, that's all anyone really needs.

The session continues, with Evelyn speaking more openly now, her voice still trembling but growing stronger with each word. She talks about the constant pressure she feels to meet expectations, about the guilt she feels when she can't live up to those expectations. She talks about her fears—fears of disappointing her parents, of letting down her friends, of not being worthy of love or success. She talks about the overwhelming sense that she is always falling short, always just not enough.

And all I can do is listen. Listen and remind her that she is enough—just as she is. That her worth is not tied to her productivity, her achievements, or how others perceive her. That she is enough simply because she exists, simply because she is a human being worthy of love and kindness, both from others and from herself.

By the end of the session, she is quieter, though the tears still linger in the corners of her eyes. She thanks me again, her voice still fragile but more certain now. She promises herself that she will take one small step toward being kinder to herself, to allowing herself to be imperfect, to not always have to be the person who holds it all together.

And I watch her walk out, her shoulders a little less hunched, her eyes a little less downcast. I hope, I pray, that she will hold on to what she's said, that she will remember that the road to healing is not about fixing everything at once, but about taking one small step at a time.

As the door clicks shut behind her, I sit there for a moment, letting the silence wash over me again. I've spent the entire session listening to Evelyn's pain, offering her the space to cry, to speak, to be heard. And yet, somehow, it feels like I am the one who has been healed, just a little.

I lean back in my chair, the tension in my body starting to release, and for the first time in a long time, I allow myself to breathe deeply. There's something powerful about simply being present for someone else, about holding space for their pain without trying to fix it.

It's not the same as healing my own wounds. It's not a cure for my own exhaustion, my own weariness. But it's a start. And maybe that's enough for now.

The next session will begin soon, and I know I'll be ready. Ready to listen, ready to guide. But this time, I will carry a small piece of this moment with me—a reminder that I am human too, that it's okay to not have all the answers, that it's okay to need help.

For the first time in a long time, I don't feel like I'm carrying it all alone. And maybe, just maybe, that is the most powerful thing of all.

The minutes slip away, almost imperceptibly, as I sit in the quiet aftermath of the session. I find myself not looking at the clock, but listening to the soft hum of my thoughts as they drift, slow and steady. Evelyn's words are still lingering in the room, like a perfume that clings to the air long after the scent is gone.

She's not the first one to come in with that same ache, that same sense of being buried under the weight of unspoken expectations. But today, something feels different. Maybe it's because I've been sitting with my own weight a little longer, allowing myself to feel that familiar ache in my chest. The ache that always comes when I think about the toll this work takes on me.

I stand up, stretching my arms overhead, trying to shake off the heaviness that's slowly creeping into my body. I've always been good at faking it, at putting on the mask and pretending that everything is fine. But today, it feels harder. Like the mask is slipping, like the cracks in the foundation are starting to show.

I walk to the window again, watching the city lights flicker to life as the night settles over the streets. The same streets I've walked a thousand times, the same streets that somehow seem to mirror my internal world—busy, filled with people, but so often silent, so often unseen.

I wonder if anyone notices me. The healer. The listener. The one who always gives but never asks for anything in return.

I lean against the window, staring out into the darkness. It's comforting, in a way, to feel the night envelop me. There's something about the night that makes everything feel a little less sharp, a little less demanding. I've often wondered if the moon, with all its quiet glow, ever feels the weight of the world. After all, it reflects the light of the sun but never shines with its own brilliance. Does it ever yearn for its own light?

The doorbell rings again. My heart jumps in my chest, but I force myself to smooth out my expression, to pull the mask back into place. I don't have the luxury of time to dwell on my own thoughts right now. Another person is waiting for me. Another soul who needs to be seen.

I open the door to reveal a man this time—a little older than the usual clients, maybe in his early forties. His eyes are tired, dark circles under them, as though he hasn't had a full night's sleep in years. He's standing a little too rigidly, like someone who's been trained to hold everything in, to never let his guard down.

"Mr. Lawson," I greet him softly, motioning for him to come in. "It's good to see you again. Please, make yourself comfortable."

He offers a strained smile, nodding as he enters and takes a seat across from me. He's dressed in a sharp suit, his posture impeccable, but there's an edge to him today—something that feels like it's on the verge of breaking.

"I've been meaning to ask," he says, his voice low, almost hesitant. "How do you do it?"

I raise an eyebrow, surprised by the question. "Do what?"

"How do you... handle it?" he continues, leaning forward slightly. "The weight of all the stories, the pain, the suffering. How do you listen to it every day and not lose yourself in it?"

I blink, caught off guard. No one has ever asked me this before. I've never stopped to think about it in such direct terms. But now, with his question hanging in the air, I realize that it's something I've never fully allowed myself to examine. I've been so focused on helping others, on guiding them through their struggles, that I've neglected to look at how it's affecting me.

I sigh, sitting back in my chair. "It's not easy," I admit, my voice quiet. "I won't pretend that it is. Every story is different, but they all leave their mark on me. In some ways, I carry them with me, whether I want to or not. But I've learned to compartmentalize, to put it aside when I need to. I do it because I believe in the work I'm doing. I believe in helping people heal, even if I can't heal myself. It's a choice I make every day."

Mr. Lawson's eyes search mine, as though trying to gauge the truth behind my words. He seems to be weighing something in his mind before speaking again.

"But doesn't it get overwhelming? The constant giving? The listening to pain, to fear, to heartache?"

I nod slowly, feeling the truth of his words resonate within me. "Yes. It does. Sometimes it feels like it's too much. Like I'm being stretched thin, like I'm giving all of myself and not leaving enough behind for me. It's a constant balancing act, trying to give and receive in equal measure. But sometimes, you give so much that there's nothing left. And that's when I feel... empty."

The word feels heavy on my tongue. Empty. A word I rarely allow myself to use. But there it is—simple, but profound.

"I think that's why I write," I continue, almost to myself. "I write because it's the only way I know how to process it. To make sense of all the things I can't fix. Writing allows me to release the weight, even if it's just for a moment."

Mr. Lawson's expression softens, and I realize he's seeing me—really seeing me—perhaps for the first time.

"You know," he says quietly, "I think you're right. We all need an outlet. We need to let the pain go somewhere, so it doesn't consume us."

I give him a faint smile, a small glimmer of understanding passing between us. "It's true. We can't carry it all. Not without breaking."

He sits back in his chair, rubbing a hand over his face, and I can tell that his own struggles are far from over. But in this moment, in this quiet exchange, we share something deeper than just words. We share the acknowledgment that healing isn't linear, that it's messy and painful, and that sometimes, the act of letting go is just as important as the act of helping others.

When the session ends, I watch Mr. Lawson leave, his footsteps heavy on the floor as he walks toward the door. As soon as it clicks shut behind him, I feel the emptiness again—the space he's left behind. It's a familiar feeling, one I've grown accustomed to. But tonight, it feels different. It feels like a quiet invitation to be present with myself.

I sit at my desk, my hand hovering over the journal again, the same one I've hidden away in the drawer. But this time, I don't feel the need to rush through the words. There's no urgency, no pressure. Just a deep, steady breath.

I let the pen glide across the page, not searching for answers, but simply allowing myself to be—just as I am. To feel everything, without judgment. To admit that I am not perfect. I don't have all the answers, and maybe I never will. But that's okay.

I am still learning. And in that, there is grace.

The night stretches on, but the weight feels a little lighter now. Maybe tomorrow I will wake up feeling stronger, or maybe I'll wake up feeling just as fragile as today. But I know now that both can exist at the same time—that I can be both the healer and the one who needs healing.

And for the first time in a long time, that feels like enough.

The last of the night slips away quietly, like a whispered secret, and I find myself still sitting at my desk, the pen in my hand, the journal resting open before me. The world outside has quieted down—only the occasional car passing by and the distant murmur of the city still awake, oblivious to the battles we fight behind closed doors.

I don't know how long I've been here, lost in my thoughts, my writing. Time seems irrelevant now. The words I've written are messy, tangled thoughts that probably make little sense, but somehow, they bring me peace. The act of putting pen to paper, of seeing my own emotions laid bare in front of me, feels like a kind of release I hadn't allowed myself in far too long.

There's something raw about being real with yourself—truly real. Not the version of myself I put on for clients, not the therapist who always knows what to say, who always has the answers. But the person underneath all of that. The one who is broken, tired, unsure. The one who is learning how to live with the weight, how to let go without losing herself.

I close the journal, the weight of it feeling strangely comforting in my hands, like holding a small piece of my soul. Maybe tomorrow I'll write more, maybe I won't. It doesn't matter. What matters is that I've allowed myself this moment. To be. To acknowledge my own humanity. And that, I think, is the beginning of healing.

The clock chimes softly, reminding me that it's late, that the world is still turning, whether I'm ready to face it or not. I turn off the light and stand, stretching my arms one last time, the weight of the day lingering in my muscles, in my mind. But it's a quieter weight now, a familiar one that's somehow easier to bear.

I walk out of my office, the silence of the house surrounding me. I let the stillness wrap around me like a blanket, a brief reprieve from the noise of the world. I know that tomorrow will come with its own challenges, its own uncertainties. I'll meet them the same way I always do—one step at a time.

But for tonight, I let myself rest.

As I settle into bed, I close my eyes and take a deep breath, letting the quiet wash over me. I am not fixed. I am not perfect. But I am enough, just as I am. And in that realization, there is a strange kind of peace.

Tomorrow, I will wake up and face the world again, ready to be the healer, ready to listen, ready to give. But for now, I give myself permission to simply be. To rest. To heal.

And with that, I close my eyes, finally letting go, if only for a little while.

II

Healer Who Hurts - Reflection

In the world of mental health and healing, there is a paradox that often goes unnoticed, especially in the case of those who dedicate their lives to helping others: the healers who hurt. These are the professionals, like therapists, counselors, and mental health advocates, who work tirelessly to support others in their darkest moments. They listen to stories of trauma, pain, grief, and struggle, offering solace, advice, and guidance. But beneath the surface of their seemingly calm, collected exteriors, many of these healers are silently bearing their own emotional burdens.

The problem lies not in their ability to help others, but in the systemic and personal challenges that arise from their role. The culture of healing often demands that the healer be strong, composed, and always available. They are expected to have all the answers, to hold space for others' pain without cracking under the weight. But the truth is far more complex. Healers are human too. They feel. They struggle. They break. And yet, the very nature of their work often demands that they repress their own emotions, leaving little room for self-care or emotional expression. This becomes a quiet crisis in the healing professions—a crisis of burnout, emotional exhaustion, and self-neglect.

This imbalance is deeply ingrained in the expectations placed on those in the healing professions. The social narrative that positions healers as unwavering, invincible figures leaves no room for the acknowledgment of their own struggles. Healers are expected to give endlessly, even when they are drained. They are expected to be unshakable, even when their foundation is crumbling beneath them. This is the definition of the problem: a society that demands constant giving from its healers, without recognizing that those who give most need care too.

The issue is subtle because it's often invisible. Healers are trained to compartmentalize, to keep their personal struggles separate from their professional lives. They are often too busy managing the pain of others to acknowledge their own. The daily emotional toll they endure doesn't come in the form of outward physical symptoms. Instead, it manifests in quiet, insidious ways—burnout, fatigue, irritability, and emotional detachment.

Evelyn, the protagonist of The Healer Who Hurts, embodies this subtlety. Her ability to empathize with and support her clients is built on years of careful self-restraint. She has learned to wear the mask of the professional—calm, collected, and always ready to help. But inside, she is falling apart. She feels herself slipping away, drowning in the weight of others' pain, with no one to help her carry it.

The issue is further exacerbated by the societal misconception of strength. The healer is seen as a symbol of resilience, as someone who must always be the rock, the anchor, the one who doesn't break. Society often neglects to recognize that true strength lies in vulnerability—being able to admit when you need help, when you are overwhelmed, and when you can't carry it all alone. The healer who hurts is a product of a society that mistakenly equates strength with silence and suffering with weakness.

In the helping professions, there is an expectation that healers must always be available for others. This is not just a professional expectation, but a cultural one. Healers are often glorified for their selflessness, praised for their dedication to the well-being of others. And yet, this very selflessness is what can slowly erode their own sense of self.

When you are always giving, always listening, always there for others, you risk losing sight of your own needs. The demands of the profession—whether it's a therapist, counselor, social worker, or mental health advocate—can often blur the lines between personal and professional life. The emotional toll of helping others cannot be measured in traditional ways. It's not about hours worked, tasks completed, or goals achieved. It's about emotional labor. It's about giving a piece of yourself in every conversation, in every session, in every moment of connection.

But what happens when there's nothing left to give? What happens when the healer has poured out every last ounce of empathy, every last drop of energy, and yet is expected to continue? The unspoken burden of this cycle is the slow, steady erosion of the healer's own well-being. Many healers struggle with guilt—the guilt that comes from taking time for themselves, from acknowledging that they need rest, from stepping away to care for their own mental health. They feel that to do so would be a failure.

This culture of constant giving is rarely questioned, but it is a flawed system. It's built on the premise that others' needs must always come first, and that the healer must sacrifice their own well-being for the sake of others. But this is unsustainable. No one can give endlessly without eventually burning out.

Dear Fellow Healers,

I see you. I see the quiet moments when you're alone with your thoughts, when the weight of it all presses down on your chest and you can't breathe. I see how you keep going, keep pushing through, because that's what we do—we help, we listen, we give. But no one tells you that it's okay to take a step back. No one tells you that you are allowed to rest, to be human, to feel the exhaustion that comes with carrying the world's pain on your shoulders.

We were trained to be strong, to be the ones people turn to when their world falls apart. But who do we turn to when our world starts to crumble? Who listens when we need to speak? Who helps us carry the weight that we so often carry alone?

You are not weak for feeling tired. You are not failing for needing a break. You are not lesser for acknowledging that you can't always be the one to fix everything. In fact, it takes immense courage to admit that you need help too. It takes strength to put down the mask and say, "I am not okay, but that doesn't make me any less worthy of love and care."

I want to remind you, as much as I remind myself, that it is okay to not be okay. It is okay to pause. It is okay to be vulnerable. It is okay to take care of yourself—because, dear healer, you cannot pour from an empty cup.

You deserve rest. You deserve compassion. You deserve a space to be heard without feeling the weight of others' pain pressing against you. You are more than your work. You are more than the healing you provide. You are a person with your own needs, your own struggles, your own dreams. And those deserve to be seen too.

So, my dear friend, take the time you need. Step away when you must. Be gentle with yourself. You are not alone. And you are not expected to carry the world on your shoulders. It is not a failure to ask for help. It is an act of self-love.

Take care of yourself. Heal yourself. Rest.

With all my heart,

Evelyn

III

The Masked Mother

The living room smelled like warm milk and lavender fabric softener. Sunlight filtered through the half-closed curtains, spilling a golden haze across the tiled floor. The house was calm—almost too calm. In the bassinet, her baby was finally asleep, one chubby fist curled next to his cheek, lips parted in the gentlest pout. A perfect baby. A miracle. Everyone said so.

Maya stared at him, her arms loose at her sides, her chest rising and falling in an oddly detached rhythm. She didn't feel like a mother. Not the kind people posted about—the radiant, soft-eyed, always-grateful kind who seemed to glow in hospital photos and wax poetic about the magic of motherhood. She felt like an actress caught in the wrong role.

Her phone buzzed next to a half-empty cup of tea. Another message in the family group: "Look at you! You were made for this, Maya. Glowing, even on two hours of sleep!"

She smiled on reflex and typed, "Haha, thank you! We're doing well, just tired." Then she tossed the phone aside, the smile fading from her face before the message had even delivered.

Her body ached. Not in the way it had after giving birth—but in a kind of slow, submerged way, like she'd been treading emotional water for days, weeks, maybe even since the moment she held her son for the first time and didn't feel that mythical lightning bolt of love. She had expected to cry happy tears. Instead, she had stared at him in stunned silence, wondering why her chest felt hollow.

No one talks about this part, she thought. The part where you lie to everyone—including yourself.

Shye walked into the kitchen and opened the fridge, forgetting what she came for. She stared blankly at the rows of prepped meals her mother-in-law had carefully packed in steel containers. Food that went uneaten most days. Hunger didn't visit her much anymore. Guilt, however, had moved in permanently.

She looked at the clock. 10:47 AM. Another day had begun and she had no idea how to fill it. The hours stretched in front of her like a long hallway with no doors, no end.

The baby stirred. Her shoulders tensed instinctively. She walked back to the bassinet and stared down at him again. He was so small, so perfect, so helpless. And all she could think was, He deserves someone better. Someone who loves him properly. Someone who doesn't have to pretend.

She heard the front door open. Her husband, back from a quick errand.

"Hey," he whispered, placing a paper bag on the counter. "He asleep?"

She nodded.

"Good. You're doing great, Maya. Seriously. You're amazing."

Her throat tightened. She nodded again, afraid that if she opened her mouth, the wrong words would fall out. No, I'm not amazing. I'm not even okay. I think something's wrong with me. I don't feel anything. I want to run.

But instead, she just whispered, "Thanks."

He kissed her cheek and disappeared into the other room. She stayed by the bassinet, watching her baby breathe. Up. Down. Up. Down. Perfectly rhythmic. Perfectly peaceful. So different from the storm that had taken up permanent residence in her mind.

She sat down slowly on the edge of the couch, her fingers trembling slightly as they hovered over her phone. She opened the camera and flipped it to selfie mode. She smiled.

Click.

A soft, glowing photo. A young mother. A picture of calm. A masked mother.

She uploaded it to her Instagram story with the caption: "Learning to love the chaos. Grateful beyond words."

She watched it post, then turned off her phone.

And quietly, she began to cry.

It started with the exhaustion.

It wasn't the kind of exhaustion that could be soothed by a nap. It was the bone-deep weariness that seemed to seep into her soul, a feeling that no amount of sleep could fix. Even when Maya managed to rest for a few hours—whether the baby was sleeping or her husband was watching over him—she woke up feeling like she hadn't closed her eyes at all.

She would lie in bed, staring at the ceiling, her hands resting over her chest as if trying to anchor herself. Each breath felt heavier than the last, each second longer than it should be. The clock ticked incessantly, mocking her inability to move. She wasn't sure what was worse: the constant weariness or the crushing weight of her own thoughts. She couldn't seem to shut them off.

She used to love mornings. She used to wake up early, full of energy, ready to meet the world with a quiet smile. Now, waking up felt like stepping into a fog. Everything seemed out of focus, like she was watching the world from behind a glass window. Her hands were always trembling, and the small tasks that had once been easy—making tea, folding clothes, picking up the baby—felt insurmountable.

It was the little things at first. The mornings when she didn't immediately feel the surge of warmth when she looked at her baby. The days when she forgot to eat, or when she ate, but didn't feel satisfied. The evenings when her husband came home from work, and she greeted him with a smile that felt like it came from a stranger's face. She would ask him how his day had been, but only half-listen to the answer, her mind spinning with thoughts she couldn't name.

The guilt came right after.

"Why can't I just be happy?" she thought, watching her husband play with their son. "Why is it so hard? I should be grateful. I should be feeling something."

Instead, she felt... nothing. Not joy. Not love. Not excitement. Only an emptiness that stretched endlessly in front of her, as if her heart had been hollowed out and replaced with quiet terror.

But the hardest part was the overwhelming sense of disconnection. It was as though she were living in a body that didn't belong to her anymore. The days blended into one another—yesterday, today, tomorrow—each indistinguishable from the next. Her body was always there, a machine that moved and fed and rocked the baby, but it wasn't her own.

Maya would stand in front of the mirror, staring at her reflection, trying to remember what it felt like to be herself. The woman she saw wasn't familiar. Her skin looked pale, her eyes tired, her smile forced. When had she last felt like Maya?

Was it before the baby? Before all the pressure to be perfect? Was it before everyone else started telling her who she should be, how she should feel?

The whispers in her head grew louder with each passing day, reminding her that she wasn't enough. Reminding her that every time she didn't feel what she was supposed to feel, she was failing.

And so, she started to fake it.

When her mother-in-law called again to check on her, Maya lied through the entire conversation. She told her everything was fine. She told her that the baby was sleeping well, that she was doing just fine, that motherhood suited her. But inside, she felt like she was sinking deeper, like she was losing herself bit by bit.

She had always been the kind of person who prided herself on her independence, on being able to handle whatever came her way. And yet now, with the baby in her arms, she felt utterly helpless. She felt like a fraud—someone playing at motherhood but never quite getting it right.

Her husband noticed the change, of course.

One evening, after a particularly grueling day, he found her sitting on the couch, staring blankly at the wall. The baby was asleep in his bassinet, but Maya's hands were still trembling slightly, like they always did now.

"Maya," he said, sitting beside her, his voice soft but concerned. "You okay? You don't seem like yourself."

She forced a smile. "I'm just tired," she said, her voice sounding hollow to her own ears. "It's been a long day."

He touched her arm gently, a silent plea for her to let him in. But Maya couldn't bring herself to open up. She couldn't bring herself to admit that she didn't know who she was anymore.

"I'm fine," she said again, this time more firmly, as if saying the words would make them true.

He didn't push her further, but he didn't leave her either. He stayed there with her, his presence a comforting weight beside her, though it felt distant. She wanted to reach out to him. She wanted to feel something, anything, but the numbness inside her kept her frozen.

Later that night, as her husband snored softly beside her, Maya lay awake, staring into the darkness. She could hear the faint sounds of the baby breathing softly in the other room. His little body, so vulnerable, so dependent on her. And yet, despite all of that, Maya couldn't feel the connection she thought she would. She didn't feel that rush of love, that protective instinct she had heard so much about. All she felt was fear—a fear that if she didn't pull herself together soon, she might lose everything.

That was the moment she realized something was wrong. Really wrong.

Her world was closing in, and she didn't know how to stop it.

The days that followed blurred into one another. Maya found herself trapped in a cycle of pretending. In the morning, she forced herself to get out of bed, wash her face, brush her hair, and smile for the baby. She took deep breaths, feeling the air fill her lungs, trying to convince herself that everything was fine.

She had stopped crying. Not because she was okay, but because she didn't have the energy left to cry anymore. She would stand in front of the mirror, numb and empty, staring at her reflection, wondering when she would finally feel like herself again. She couldn't find the answer.

She couldn't even recognize the woman in the mirror anymore. Was she a mother? A wife? A person?

There was a new woman inside her, one she didn't understand. She was quieter, more withdrawn, more afraid. She was starting to feel like a ghost, an echo of the person she used to be.

The more she thought about it, the more she realized something: she hadn't asked for help. Not really. Not truly. Not in a way that might make a difference.

She knew the signs of postpartum depression. She'd read about it in books, heard about it from other mothers, seen it discussed on social media. But it was always one of those things that happened to other people, not to someone like her. Someone who had always prided herself on being strong, self-sufficient, able to handle anything life threw her way.

But now she was drowning, and she couldn't pretend anymore.

It was a quiet Tuesday afternoon when she decided to Google the words: "postpartum depression symptoms."

She clicked on the first link and began to read, her heart racing as the words appeared on the screen. The list of symptoms felt like a checklist of everything she'd been silently battling for weeks—anxiety, guilt, emotional numbness, irritability, a disconnection from her baby, overwhelming sadness that she couldn't explain. She could feel the weight of the words pressing down on her, the truth settling into her bones.

"I'm not crazy," she whispered to herself, her hands shaking. "I'm not alone. This is real."

She didn't know what she had expected—maybe just a confirmation that she was doing it wrong, that she wasn't cut out for motherhood. But reading the words on the screen made her realize that this wasn't a matter of not being good enough. This was something that happened. It was a medical condition, and it was real.

But knowing that didn't make it any easier. She still felt scared. She still felt ashamed. How could she, someone who had always prided herself on handling challenges, be sick in this way?

The stigma, the shame—it was suffocating.

That evening, as her husband was giving the baby a bath, Maya found herself sitting on the edge of the couch, staring at her phone. The number to a therapist's office was right there in front of her. It had been there for days, weeks even. She had saved it, telling herself she'd call when she was ready, but never doing it. The fear had kept her frozen. What would they think of her? Would they judge her for not being able to handle it? Would they see her as weak?

Her finger hovered over the phone screen, the weight of the decision heavy in her chest. For a moment, she considered letting it go. It was just a phase, right? She could power through it. She could be strong. She had always been strong.

But then she remembered the way she had felt that night, lying in bed, her mind spinning with fear. She remembered the hollow feeling inside her, the emptiness that had never gone away. She remembered the deep, quiet terror that had been growing, and she realized something else:

She didn't want to stay like this. She didn't want to live like this anymore.

With a deep breath, she finally pressed the number. The phone rang. She held it to her ear, her heart pounding in her chest.

"Hello?" a voice answered on the other end.

"I—I need help," Maya whispered, her voice barely audible. "I think I have postpartum depression."

The words felt strange as they left her mouth. But they were true. And that truth, though terrifying, felt like the first step toward something better.

The next few weeks were a mix of therapy sessions, long conversations with her husband, and an overwhelming amount of self-reflection. At first, it felt like the weight on her shoulders only grew heavier as she began to confront the depth of her struggles. Every session with her therapist brought up new emotions—guilt, fear, shame—and she didn't always know how to handle them.

But slowly, little by little, something shifted inside her. She began to understand that the depression wasn't her fault. She wasn't weak. She wasn't failing. She was healing.

The more she spoke about her experiences, the more she started to feel understood, seen, and—perhaps most importantly—valid. Her therapist reassured her that what she was experiencing was normal for many mothers, that it didn't make her any less of a woman or a mother.

Her husband was learning too. He was trying his best to understand her, to be present, to help in ways that didn't feel like he was pushing her. He took the baby for longer walks, gave her space to rest, and reminded her, time and time again, that she wasn't alone in this. He didn't expect her to be perfect. He didn't need her to be.

It wasn't easy. It wasn't quick. But Maya began to see the faintest light at the end of the tunnel.

One day, while playing with her baby on the living room floor, she felt it. The tiniest flicker of something inside her. It wasn't the overwhelming love she'd imagined, but it was something—something more than the numbness that had defined the last few months. It was a small connection. A tiny step toward feeling whole again.

And for the first time in months, she allowed herself to believe that it was okay to take it one day at a time. That she didn't have to be perfect. That healing was a journey—and that, for once, she didn't have to face it alone.

The hardest part was always the silence.

Maya's therapy sessions were opening doors she'd long kept locked, but the walls she had built up outside of those four safe walls were still standing tall. She could say the words in therapy—postpartum depression, exhaustion, guilt, fear—but outside that room, the words felt foreign and dangerous. They didn't belong in the world outside, where everything was supposed to be perfect. Where she was supposed to be a glowing new mother, the picture of happiness and fulfillment.

But Maya was learning something important in therapy: the truth was messy. It didn't always fit the image people expected. And yet, even as the pieces of her healing began to fit together, there was still a part of her that felt like a failure for not being able to share her truth with anyone else.

Her mom called a few days after her first therapy session. Maya hesitated before picking up, the phone vibrating in her hand like it was a test she wasn't sure she wanted to take. It was early in the morning, the baby was napping, and Maya had just finished her cup of tea, something that had become a small ritual to help calm her nerves.

"Maya," her mother's voice came through the line, warm but chipper, "how are you, darling? I hope everything is going well with the baby."

"I'm fine, Mom. Everything is… good." She forced the words out, feeling them stick in her throat.

Her mother's voice softened. "You know, I remember when you were born. Your father and I didn't have a lot of help back then, and we just did it. Your grandmother never complained, you know. She was always so strong. I'm sure you're doing the same."

Maya's chest tightened, and for a moment, she didn't know how to respond. There was a heaviness in her that she couldn't share. She couldn't tell her mom that she didn't feel strong. That some days, she could barely get out of bed, let alone play the part of the strong, capable mother that her family and society expected.

"I'm doing okay, Mom," she said again, but this time, her voice cracked. It wasn't much, but it was enough for her mother to hear.

"Good, good. Just make sure you're eating, okay? And don't be afraid to ask for help if you need it. But you're doing great, honey. You always do." Her mother's voice trailed off, leaving a familiar weight behind. It was a sweet, well-meaning sentiment, but it felt like a pat on the back, an attempt to sweep everything under the rug without really seeing what Maya was going through.

Her mother hung up after a few more pleasantries, and Maya sat there, staring at the phone in her hand, feeling a knot form in her stomach.

What if I told her? What if I said that I'm not okay? What if I admitted that I'm not handling this as well as I should?

Would she still love me? Would she understand?

She didn't know. And that fear, the fear of being misunderstood or of being seen as weak, kept her silent.

Later that evening, as Maya sat on the couch, nursing the baby in the soft light of their living room, her husband, Sam, came in with a cup of tea. He had been trying, she could feel it. Trying to be patient, trying to help, trying to understand. But every time he asked how she was doing, every time he reached out, Maya pulled away, not knowing how to explain the quiet chaos inside her.

"Hey, how's he doing?" Sam asked, his voice gentle as he sat beside her on the couch, looking at their son. "He's been a little fussy all day, but I think it's just the teething. You look tired. You're sure you're okay?"

Maya opened her mouth, ready to say something—anything—but the words wouldn't come. What would she say? That she felt disconnected? That she felt like a stranger in her own body? That she was scared she wasn't doing this right, that she couldn't give him the kind of love he deserved?

She closed her eyes, swallowing the lump in her throat. The last time they had talked about her feelings, he had been supportive, but she hadn't been honest. She hadn't told him the full truth. She hadn't said how alone she felt, even when he was right beside her.

"I'm okay, Sam," she said softly. "I just... I'm really tired."

He gave her a sideways look, his brows furrowing slightly, but he didn't press her. Instead, he placed the cup of tea on the coffee table and gently rubbed her back. She appreciated the gesture, but it only made her feel more fragile. Her eyes burned with the urge to cry, but she forced herself to swallow it back down.

"You know, you don't have to do everything on your own, right?" Sam said, his voice low, sincere. "I'm here. You can tell me anything."

The words were kind. They were comforting. And yet, they didn't ease the crushing feeling in her chest.

"I know," Maya whispered, finally meeting his eyes. She tried to smile, but it came out more like a grimace. "I'm just... not sure how to talk about it."

Sam squeezed her shoulder, clearly not understanding but still trying his best. "You don't have to have all the answers. I'm here. Just... let me know what you need. We're in this together."

Maya wanted to believe him. She wanted to lean into his words, to let him in fully. But there was a barrier inside her that she couldn't quite break through. A wall she had built up over the years, brick by brick. A wall that told her, If you let people see the real you, they'll think you're weak. They'll think you're failing.

So instead, she nodded, even though a small voice in the back of her mind whispered, This isn't enough. This silence isn't enough.

The next morning, as Maya scrolled through social media during a rare moment of peace while the baby napped, she found herself drawn to a post by another mother. It was a vulnerable, raw post about struggling with postpartum depression, about not feeling enough, about the guilt of not immediately bonding with the baby. The comments below were full of other mothers sharing their own stories, their own struggles. Maya paused, her heart racing as she read through the words, recognizing herself in them.

For the first time in weeks, she felt the stirring of something deep inside her—hope. Maybe this could be the place where she could finally speak the truth, even if it wasn't face-to-face.

She sat for a long time, fingers hovering over the keyboard. She wanted to comment, to share her own story, but the fear quickly flooded in. Would people judge her? Would they call her weak, fragile, a bad mother?

She typed a few words, then deleted them. It's not worth it, she thought. It's better to stay quiet.

But as she closed the app and put her phone down, she couldn't shake the nagging thought. Maybe it's time to stop hiding.

The days after Maya's virtual conversation felt like an internal tug-of-war. On one hand, the silence that had kept her safe—protected her from judgment, from people's expectations—was suffocating her. On the other hand, the fear of speaking out, of fully unveiling her vulnerability, still loomed over her like an immovable shadow.

She thought about the comments on the post she had read, all the other mothers opening up about their own battles with postpartum depression. Some of them had said things that hit her deeply, things she had felt but hadn't been able to articulate. There was a kind of power in their words, a collective strength that made her feel less alone. And yet, the idea of stepping into that space herself—of admitting out loud that she was struggling—felt like standing on the edge of a cliff, ready to jump into an unknown abyss.

The quiet resistance was always there. The thoughts would rise up every time she considered sharing more. You'll be judged. You'll seem weak. They'll see you as incapable, a failure. Who are you to complain when so many women are doing just fine?

But the more she thought about it, the more she realized the truth: she wasn't doing just fine. And pretending to be fine wasn't helping. It was only making everything worse.

Maya was sitting at the kitchen table one evening, scrolling through her phone again, when the flood of emotions hit. She was alone. Sam had taken the baby out for a walk, giving her a rare moment of peace. For the first time in days, she allowed herself to sit with the uncomfortable feelings she had been pushing away. She took a deep breath, feeling the tightness in her chest.

She needed to talk to someone.

Not Sam. Not her mom. They were good, well-meaning people, but there were things she couldn't say to them yet. She needed to talk to someone who could understand without judgment, someone who wouldn't rush to fix her.

That was when she thought of the support group her therapist had mentioned—an online space for mothers dealing with postpartum depression. It had been sitting in the back of her mind, but she had been too afraid to check it out. Now, with her emotions threatening to overflow, she knew it was time.

She opened the app. Her fingers hovered over the search bar, her heart pounding. This was it—the moment when everything could change.

She found the group. It was private, members-only, and the posts were raw and unfiltered. She read through a few before summoning the courage to post her own message. Her hands were shaking as she typed:

"Hi. I'm new here. I've been struggling with postpartum depression, and I feel like I'm losing myself. Some days I feel like I'm doing okay, but most days... it's like I'm drowning. I don't know how to talk to anyone about it. I don't want to be judged. I don't know what to do."

She sat there, staring at the screen, waiting. What if no one replied? What if they thought she was just seeking attention, or worse, that she wasn't strong enough to be a mother? She hit send before she could talk herself out of it.

It felt like she had jumped off that cliff. The uncertainty was terrifying, but there was something liberating about finally being honest—about saying out loud what she had been hiding for so long.

She set the phone down, rubbing her temples. The quiet in the house felt heavy, like the calm before a storm.

Her phone buzzed fifteen minutes later. Maya's heart skipped a beat as she picked it up, bracing herself for the worst. But as she scrolled through the replies, her breath caught.

"I feel exactly the same way."

"I haven't told anyone either. I'm terrified of what they'll think of me."

"You're not alone. I've been through it, and I'm here to listen. It gets better, but you don't have to do it alone."

Maya's throat tightened as tears welled in her eyes. The messages were simple, but they were filled with such understanding, such compassion. She wasn't alone. There were other women who had walked this path, who had felt the same emptiness, the same fear.

She wasn't broken. She was human.

One message in particular stood out to her:

"It's okay to not be okay. It doesn't make you less of a mother, and it doesn't make you weak. You're allowed to feel how you feel. Healing takes time, and it's okay to take that time."

Maya's chest tightened, but this time, it wasn't from fear—it was from the overwhelming relief of feeling understood, of not being judged. She typed a quick reply:

"Thank you. I didn't know how much I needed to hear that. I thought I was the only one."

She sat back in her chair, breathing deeply for the first time in what felt like forever. She had taken a step—no matter how small it seemed—and for the first time, she didn't feel like she was carrying the weight of the world alone.

The next few days were filled with a different kind of quiet. Maya didn't have all the answers, and the pressure wasn't gone, but something had shifted. The thoughts of shame and fear still crept in from time to time, but they didn't have the same power over her. She had broken the silence, and in doing so, she had begun to heal.

There was a particular moment the following week, when Sam was on the couch, flipping through a book and the baby was napping in her arms. Maya took a deep breath and looked over at him. Her thoughts had been swirling—she'd been thinking a lot about the stigma, about the conversation she never had with him.

"Sam," she said quietly, her voice hesitant but determined, "I need to talk to you about something."

He put his book down, giving her his full attention. "Anything, babe. What's going on?"

Maya's voice wavered for a moment. She felt vulnerable, but she knew this was the next step in her healing. She was ready to be honest with him, to stop hiding.

"I'm struggling more than I've been letting on," she began, her eyes meeting his. "I thought I could handle it, but... I'm not okay. Not yet. I feel like I'm constantly pretending, like I'm faking it. And I don't know how to do this alone."

There was a long pause as Sam looked at her, his face softening with understanding. "Maya... why didn't you tell me? I want to be here for you, for everything. You don't have to carry this by yourself."

Her heart ached at the sincerity in his voice. She hadn't realized how much she had been holding back, how much of this journey she had kept to herself. But now, with his words, she felt the barrier finally begin to crumble.

"I didn't want to seem weak," she admitted. "I didn't want you to think I couldn't handle it."

"You don't have to be perfect, Maya," Sam said, his voice thick with emotion. "I love you. And I'm with you in this. Always."

Maya felt a tear slip down her cheek, but this time, it wasn't out of sadness. It was the release of everything she had been holding inside for so long. The silence had kept her trapped, but now, the words were free. She wasn't alone. She wasn't broken. She was healing, one conversation at a time.

Weeks had passed since Maya first opened up. There were still moments when the shadows of doubt crept in—when the overwhelming wave of guilt hit her again, when she felt that familiar sense of inadequacy claw at her heart. But each time it came, she remembered something she had read in the support group: Healing doesn't mean you'll never feel pain again. It just means you've learned how to live with it.

Maya had slowly started to embrace this new understanding. Healing was messy. It wasn't a linear process. Some days, she felt like she was moving forward, and others, she felt stuck. But she was moving nonetheless. And that, in itself, was enough.

It wasn't just the online support group that had helped. Sam's support had been invaluable, even though it hadn't been perfect. He wasn't always sure what to say, and sometimes, his attempts to make her feel better only made her feel more frustrated. But the fact that he was there—truly present, without judgment—meant everything to her.

One afternoon, Sam came home from work and found Maya sitting at the kitchen table, scribbling in a journal. The baby was napping peacefully in the crib. For the first time in weeks, she felt a sense of clarity. The journal had become a tool for her to unpack her thoughts, and while it didn't always give her answers, it helped her organize the chaos in her mind.

"Hey," Sam said softly, walking over and gently kissing her on the forehead. "How's it going?"

Maya closed the journal, a small smile tugging at her lips. "Better," she said, surprising herself. "I think I'm starting to understand that I don't have to do it all. I can ask for help. I can let myself be... human."

Sam's eyes softened, and he sat down next to her. "I'm proud of you," he said. "For everything. For being honest with me. For taking the steps to take care of yourself."

Maya leaned back in her chair, exhaling slowly. "It's been hard. I thought I could do it all by myself. I thought I had to be perfect. But... I'm learning that I don't have to be. And that's okay."

The following weekend, Maya made the decision to have the conversation she had been avoiding—the one with her mother. Her mom had always been a pillar of strength in her life, and Maya feared that admitting she wasn't okay would somehow disappoint her. But now, after months of therapy, self-reflection, and the support of Sam, Maya felt ready.

She called her mom on a Saturday morning, the phone feeling heavier than usual in her hand.

"Hi, Mom," Maya greeted, her voice steady but soft.

"Maya, darling! How are you? How's my grandbaby?"

"He's doing well," Maya replied, a small smile forming at the mention of her son. "Actually, there's something I need to talk to you about."

Her mother's tone shifted, concern creeping in. "Of course, honey. What's going on?"

Maya took a deep breath. "I've been struggling, Mom. I don't think I've been completely honest with you."

There was a long pause on the other end. Her mother's voice softened. "What do you mean?"

"I've been dealing with postpartum depression," Maya confessed, her voice trembling slightly. "And I've been really hard on myself, thinking I had to do it all. But I'm not okay. And I've been hiding that from you... from everyone."

Her mother's voice grew quiet, the words coming out slower, as if she were processing the weight of what Maya had just shared. "Oh, darling... Why didn't you say anything sooner?"

"I didn't want to disappoint you," Maya whispered, the confession hanging between them. "I thought I should be stronger. That I should have it all together."

"Oh, sweetheart," her mother said, her voice filled with warmth. "You don't have to be perfect. I wish you had told me. I would've been here for you. You're not alone in this. You've always had my love and support, no matter what."

Maya felt a wave of relief wash over her. For the first time in a long while, she didn't feel like she had to hide her struggles behind a mask. She wasn't perfect, but that didn't change the love she had for her family or the love they had for her.

As the months passed, Maya continued to find small victories. The silence that once consumed her was now filled with words—words of truth, vulnerability, and healing. She began to recognize the strength in her own vulnerability and the power that came from asking for help.

Therapy sessions were still a part of her routine, but they didn't feel as overwhelming anymore. She was no longer walking into them feeling like she had to pretend to be "fine." She was learning to be honest with herself, and that honesty extended to the people she loved.

She also found herself more present with her son, savoring the quiet moments together instead of feeling like she was constantly behind, always trying to catch up. There were still hard days, but Maya had learned that those days didn't define her. They were just moments in a much bigger journey.

Sam continued to be her rock, and she found herself leaning into his support in ways she hadn't before. They talked more openly about their relationship, their hopes, and their struggles. Maya learned that it was okay to lean on him, just as he leaned on her.

One night, as Maya lay in bed with Sam, the baby sleeping peacefully in the crib across the room, she reflected on everything she had learned. She had spent so many years trying to be the perfect daughter, wife, and mother. But the truth was, there was no such thing as perfect. What made her strong wasn't her ability to always be put together—it was her willingness to be vulnerable, to admit when she needed help, and to seek out the support she deserved.

She reached over, taking Sam's hand in hers. He squeezed it gently.

"Thank you," she whispered, her voice thick with emotion. "Thank you for being here with me. I know I haven't always been easy."

He chuckled softly. "You don't have to thank me, Maya. I'm just glad you're here with me."

"I think I'm starting to get it," Maya said, her voice steady now. "That strength doesn't mean doing it all. It means letting go of the pressure to be perfect and just... being human."

Sam smiled, brushing a lock of hair away from her face. "You've always been strong, Maya. And I'm proud of you for realizing that."

And as Maya lay there in the quiet of the night, with the soft, rhythmic sound of her son's breathing in the background, she knew that the road ahead wouldn't be easy. But it would be her road. And she wasn't walking it alone.

IV

The Masked Mother - Reflection

Postpartum depression (PPD) is a mental health condition that can affect women after childbirth. Unlike the temporary sadness or mood swings that many mothers experience in the first few days following delivery (often referred to as the "baby blues"), PPD is a deeper, more persistent feeling of sadness, hopelessness, and emotional numbness that lasts much longer—weeks, months, or even a year. It can have a significant impact on a mother's ability to care for herself and her baby, creating an emotional and psychological distance between the two.

For Maya, it wasn't just a sense of sadness; it was an overwhelming sense of disconnection. She felt like a stranger in her own life—like she was watching her motherhood from a distance, unable to fully engage or connect with her son. It was a constant, nagging feeling that no matter how hard she tried, she was never enough.

Maya never imagined that after giving birth to her son, she would be navigating a world filled with so much hidden pain. She had heard of the "baby blues," the fatigue that followed childbirth, and the fleeting mood swings mothers often experienced. But no one had warned her about what could come after—the overwhelming, persistent weight of postpartum depression (PPD). For months, Maya assumed it was just part of the process, something she had to endure in silence. She didn't realize until much later that she wasn't alone in these feelings, nor was she weak for experiencing them.

Postpartum depression is often misunderstood, and for many mothers, it goes undiagnosed or misdiagnosed. For Maya, it was like a quiet storm building inside her—a storm that wasn't obvious to the outside world, but one that threatened to consume her from the inside.

Emotional numbness: This is one of the most insidious symptoms. It doesn't always look like sadness. Often, it manifests as emotional detachment—feeling numb or indifferent to things you once cared about. Maya found it difficult to feel joy in moments she should have cherished.

Common Symptoms of PPD:

Guilt: A pervasive feeling of inadequacy. No matter what she did, Maya couldn't shake the feeling that she was failing. She couldn't meet the expectations of what a "good" mother was supposed to be. This guilt weighed heavily on her—why couldn't she just be happy with her baby? What was wrong with her?

Hopelessness: A sense that things would never get better. That this overwhelming sadness and exhaustion would be her life, forever. Maya would often find herself looking at her son and wondering if she was even cut out for motherhood. Would she ever feel like herself again?

Disconnection from the baby: This was one of the hardest things for Maya to admit to herself. She loved her son, but there were moments when she felt like a stranger to him. She couldn't always find the connection she had imagined would come so naturally. She would stare at his small face and wonder why it was so hard to bond.

Insomnia: Sleep became a luxury Maya couldn't afford. The physical exhaustion of caring for a newborn combined with the mental toll of PPD kept her awake at night, staring at the ceiling, unable to rest. She could never seem to sleep enough, and when she did sleep, it was often interrupted by nightmares or anxious thoughts.

Appetite changes: Whether it was eating too much to soothe her pain or losing her appetite altogether, food became something she couldn't manage. Some days, Maya found herself turning to food for comfort, mindlessly eating, while on others, she struggled to force down even a few bites.

These symptoms don't just appear in isolation; they compound each other. The guilt leads to feelings of hopelessness. The exhaustion makes the emotional numbness even harder to bear. All of this can lead a mother to feel isolated, misunderstood, and afraid to speak out about what she's experiencing.

Why PPD Goes Undiagnosed?

Despite how common PPD is—affecting one in every seven mothers—so many women suffer in silence. For Maya, the idea of speaking out about her struggles felt almost impossible. There were so many reasons she hesitated to ask for help, even as she felt herself slipping further away from the life she had known.

One of the most insidious factors in this silence is the stigma surrounding mental health. In many cultures, especially those with strong traditional values like Maya's, mental illness—especially depression—is often seen as something shameful. There's a pervasive belief that mothers, in particular, should be able to "bounce back" after childbirth. They are expected to be happy, glowing, and overflowing with joy as they care for their babies. To admit that they are struggling feels like an admission of failure. It means acknowledging that they are not perfect—that they don't have it all together. In a society where perfection is often demanded, seeking help can feel like a personal defeat.

Another issue is the romanticization of motherhood. From movies to social media, the image of motherhood is often portrayed as an idealistic experience—a blissful bond between mother and child. But the reality is far messier. While there are beautiful moments, there are also moments of exhaustion, frustration, and even resentment. These are the aspects of motherhood that no one talks about because they don't fit the narrative of the "perfect mom." This silence around the less-than-perfect moments leaves mothers like Maya feeling ashamed to speak out, to ask for help.

Why Asking for Help Isn't Weakness—it's Courage

As Maya continued her journey through PPD, she came to understand something profoundly important: asking for help was not a sign of weakness. In fact, it was an act of great courage.

At first, Maya struggled with the idea of reaching out to others. She didn't want to be a burden to her friends or family. But as she spoke with other mothers—through the support group and with Sam—she began to see the truth: everyone needs support. No one can navigate such a monumental life transition alone. The act of opening up to others, of letting them see the parts of yourself that are hurting, is an incredible act of strength. It's saying, "I can't do this alone, and that's okay."

Maya learned that strength comes from vulnerability. It comes from showing up in the midst of struggle and saying, "I need help. I'm not okay, and that's okay too." It's about releasing the pressure to be perfect and embracing the humanity of motherhood.

Learning to Show Up As She Is

Maya still has hard days. Some mornings, she wakes up and feels like the weight of the world is pressing down on her chest. Other times, the feelings of guilt and shame creep in again, whispering that she's not doing enough for her baby. But every day, she's learning to show up, not as who she thinks she should be, but as she truly is—a mother who is doing her best, even in the face of struggles.

Maya is learning to accept that there is no such thing as perfection in motherhood. There are good days, and there are bad days, but each one is a step forward. And she doesn't have to walk this path alone.

Dear Mama,

I want you to know that if you are struggling, if you feel alone, if you feel like you're failing—you are not. I see you. I understand. And I am here to tell you that what you are feeling is valid. You are not weak for having hard days. You are not alone in your pain.

Motherhood is hard. It's messy, overwhelming, and beautiful all at once. And it's okay to not have it all figured out. It's okay to ask for help. It's okay to admit that you're not okay. I know how hard it is to take that first step—to acknowledge that you need support—but trust me, it's one of the most powerful things you can do for yourself and your baby.

So, to all the mothers out there, especially the ones who feel like they're drowning in silence, I want you to hear me: You are doing enough. You are enough. And there is no shame in seeking help.

Keep going, even on the days when you feel like giving up. You are not alone. We are in this together.

With love and solidarity,

—Maya

V
The Teenage Warrior

Sanya's phone buzzed beside her, pulling her from the haze of sleep. The cold light from the screen flooded her dark room, illuminating her face like the start of another performance. She squinted at the notifications that blinked, one after another, like a chorus of voices calling her name. The usual mix: a few likes here, a comment there. But what stood out was the notification from her school's group chat. "Sanya, you crushed it on that chemistry test! Everyone's talking about it. We're lucky to have you in the class!"

Her fingers moved automatically, scrolling through the messages, her thumb pausing on the photo she'd posted the night before—a perfectly staged shot of her study space, her notes neatly arranged beside a steaming cup of herbal tea. The caption: "Late-night grind. #StudyingHard #FutureGoals."

It had only been up for a few hours, but the likes were already in the hundreds, the comments pouring in, a validation that felt both good and... empty. A hollow kind of satisfaction.

"Here we go again," she muttered under her breath, tossing the phone aside. But the glow from the screen still lingered in her mind, as if it was an unshakable shadow that clung to her. She could almost hear the voices of her followers, the voices of her classmates, even the ones who didn't know her, telling her that she was doing it right, that she was the one who had it all together. She was the perfect student, the perfect friend, the perfect daughter. But no one saw the cracks. No one saw the chaos that lived just behind her smile.

Sanya had been told her whole life that she was capable of greatness. Her parents, her teachers, even strangers, had all pointed to her as the golden child—the one who would go on to do amazing things. They saw her perfect grades, her carefully curated friendships, and her ever-present confidence. What they didn't see was the knot of anxiety that twisted her stomach each time she sat down to study, the sleepless nights spent wondering if today's achievement would be enough to meet the impossible standards she had set for herself. What they didn't see was how, for every piece of praise, she felt a little more like an imposter.

The mask had been put on so long ago that it was starting to feel like part of her. It was an intricate piece, made up of perfect grades, impeccable style, a tightly-knit friend group, and flawless social media. And yet, every day, the pressure to maintain it grew heavier.

Sanya pulled herself out of bed, quickly throwing on her uniform—a skirt that sat just above her knees, a shirt neatly tucked in, the fabric ironed to perfection. It was a routine, a ritual. She moved through it like a robot, always checking the clock, always rushing, always making sure everything appeared as it should. She caught a glimpse of herself in the mirror as she passed by. The face staring back at her seemed familiar, yet foreign. The flawless skin, the well-groomed hair, the slight tilt of her head—it all looked so perfect. "You look great today," she told herself, her voice sounding almost robotic. But beneath that smile, her eyes betrayed her. They were tired. She was tired.

At school, it was the same story. The same smiles, the same compliments, the same perfectly measured responses. She excelled in every subject, participated in every extracurricular, and still managed to hang out with her friends on weekends. To the outside world, Sanya was untouchable. She was the girl everyone wanted to be—smart, beautiful, confident. But she wasn't real. Not the way they saw her.

In the lunchroom, she sat with her friends, a group that seemed so perfectly coordinated it could have been designed by a stylist. The girls in her group all had the same vibe: effortlessly chic, effortlessly popular. They laughed at jokes, swapped stories, and posted group photos that were always picture-perfect.

As they chatted, Sanya's eyes flicked to her phone, which sat on the table beside her. The screen was still filled with notifications. Another new post was up: this time from Aarohi, the classmate who was always the center of attention. Aarohi had posted a picture from last night's party—a picture where she looked like she'd stepped out of a magazine. Sanya felt a twinge in her chest. Aarohi was effortlessly stunning. Her hair looked like it had been professionally styled, her skin was radiant, and her eyes sparkled with that kind of carefree joy that Sanya could never quite replicate. The caption was simple: "Live in the moment. #LivingMyBestLife"

And there it was—the perfect life. The kind of life Sanya could never seem to achieve, even though, by all accounts, she was doing everything right. The tug of comparison settled deep in her chest. The tight knot of insecurity coiled, making her fingers itch to check her feed again. She could already see the likes on her latest post stacking up, but it didn't matter. Why didn't it matter?

Her friend Meera noticed her distracted gaze and nudged her. "Hey, everything okay? You're not your usual self today."

Sanya snapped out of her reverie. "Yeah, just tired," she said, forcing a smile that didn't quite reach her eyes. "I've got a lot to catch up on tonight."

"Well, you're killing it as usual," Meera said, her voice full of admiration.

Sanya nodded, but inside, she could feel the weight of those words bearing down on her. Killing it. Was she? Or was she just pretending to be?

At that moment, Sanya excused herself from the table. She didn't want to talk anymore, didn't want to pretend. She needed a moment, a break from the facade. She slipped into the restroom, locking herself in a stall, leaning against the cool tiles. The sound of the school hallway muffled in the background, leaving her alone with her thoughts. The tears came unbidden, hot and angry. She wiped them away quickly, but they kept coming, each one a reminder of how impossible it was to keep up with the mask she had created.

She glanced at herself in the mirror above the sink. The reflection staring back at her was someone she didn't recognize—a girl who was trying to do everything right but was slowly losing herself in the process.

What's wrong with me? she thought. Why isn't this enough?

Her phone buzzed again, pulling her from her spiral. It was a message from her mother, reminding her to call after school. "Don't forget to check in, darling. We're so proud of you."

Sanya stared at the screen for a long moment, her heart heavy with guilt. Her parents expected so much from her. Everyone did. But no one knew what it cost her to keep up the appearance of perfection. No one knew how much it hurt to pretend she was okay when all she wanted to do was scream.

The phone buzzed again, a reminder of the world outside waiting for her—her friends, her classmates, her social media following, all expecting the version of Sanya that they knew. The perfect, polished Sanya.

But who was she, really?

With a sigh, Sanya wiped her face, stood up, and took a deep breath. She would go back to the lunchroom. She would smile. She would laugh. She would keep it all together for a little while longer. But deep down, she knew that sooner or later, the mask would crack. And when it did, she would have to decide who she really was, beyond the likes, beyond the achievements, beyond the pressure to be perfect.

Sanya walked back to the lunchroom, her footsteps quiet against the cold tile floor. The buzzing of her phone still echoed in her ears, like an incessant drumbeat that refused to let her forget the life she was supposed to be living. The mask was back in place now—her shoulders squared, her expression neutral but polite. She pasted on a smile, the kind that everyone expected. The kind that everyone loved.

She slid into her seat, her friends none the wiser. They were talking about weekend plans, gossiping about the latest school drama, and cracking jokes. The laughter rang in her ears like a distant sound, as if she was hearing it from far away, like she was watching a show instead of living it.

"Hey, Sanya, we're going out this Saturday, right?" Meera asked, her eyes shining with excitement. "It's going to be epic! You in?"

Sanya forced herself to smile. "Of course," she said, her voice steady. "I wouldn't miss it."

But in the back of her mind, she was already calculating the hours she'd need to study, the homework that loomed over her like a dark cloud. A part of her wanted to be free of it all, to escape, but another part of her felt paralyzed by the thought of letting go. If she let go, if she stopped being perfect, what would happen? Would people still like her? Would they still admire her? Would she even have anything left?

Her phone buzzed again. This time, it was a message from her classmate, Kunal, with a link to a blog post about "How to Manage Stress Like a Pro." She clicked on it out of curiosity.

The article was a list of tips: exercise, eat well, meditate, plan ahead, stay positive, and never forget to take breaks. She read the list, but each piece of advice felt like a cruel joke. Exercise? She barely had time to sleep, let alone hit the gym. Eat well? She subsisted on late-night snacks and coffee. Meditate? Who had time for that when there was a stack of assignments waiting for her at home?

At the end of the article, there was a quote that seemed to haunt her: "Perfection is not a goal; it's a cycle. And if you keep chasing it, you will eventually lose yourself."

Sanya sat back in her chair, the words echoing in her mind like a haunting refrain. Lose yourself. She had been so focused on being everything to everyone that she had forgotten what it felt like to be just herself. The thought of it scared her, because she didn't even know who that person was anymore.

Lunch was over before she realized it. The bell rang, and her friends stood up, chatting about the rest of their day. Sanya followed them to class, mechanically nodding and responding to their conversation. The motions felt like a script she had memorized, but it was starting to feel hollow.

In class, Sanya sat at her desk, her head bent over her notebook as she took notes. The words blurred together, her thoughts scattered. She wasn't really there, not fully. She was somewhere else—inside her own head, trapped in the whirlwind of expectations and pressures that never seemed to stop spinning.

Her mind drifted back to the moment in the bathroom. The tears she had wiped away so quickly. The frustration. The anger. The fear. But also, the deep, gnawing desire to be seen, not for her grades or her Instagram feed, but for who she was beneath all of that.

She longed for someone to look at her and say, "It's okay to not have it all together." But who could she turn to? Who could she trust with this version of herself—the version that wasn't perfect?

After school, Sanya made her way to the library to study, as she always did. The quiet hum of the room was soothing, the rows of books a comforting reminder of her constant pursuit of knowledge. But even here, she couldn't escape the pressure. The weight of her to-do list loomed over her, pulling at her focus like an anchor dragging her down.

She glanced around the room. Everyone else was so focused—so together—and Sanya couldn't help but wonder if she was the only one who felt like she was sinking under the weight of it all. The truth was, she was tired. So tired.

Her phone buzzed again. This time, it was a notification from her mom. "Just wanted to remind you how proud we are of you. Keep up the good work!"

Sanya stared at the message, the words feeling warm but distant. She could feel the pressure building again. She was doing everything she was supposed to do—she was getting good grades, keeping up with her responsibilities, posting the perfect photos—but was it really enough?

What was she really working toward? And who was she doing it for?

As the afternoon sun streamed through the library windows, Sanya made a decision. She needed to stop pretending. At least, for a moment. She couldn't keep up the perfect facade forever. Maybe it was time to admit that she wasn't okay—that she was struggling. And maybe, just maybe, it was time to let go of the idea that she had to be perfect all the time.

With a deep breath, Sanya turned off her phone, closed her notebook, and stood up from the desk. For the first time that day, she didn't feel the need to rush. She walked out of the library, not knowing what would come next, but knowing that something had to change.

She didn't have all the answers. But maybe, just maybe, it was time to stop pretending she did.

As she stepped out into the late afternoon light, she felt the first hint of relief—a small crack in the mask that had defined her for so long. She wasn't perfect. And maybe, for the first time in a long while, that was okay.

The journey was just beginning.

Sanya walked through the school gates, the weight on her shoulders feeling just a little bit lighter, though still present. The afternoon sunlight bathed everything in a soft, golden glow, and for the first time in ages, she let herself just be. She didn't rush to check her phone, didn't worry about what people would think, and didn't try to force herself into the mold of the "perfect" student everyone had come to expect.

It was strange, this quiet relief that crept up on her, as though she were stepping into a new world, one where the pressure wasn't as suffocating. She walked slowly, breathing in the air, noticing the little things she had missed—the way the trees swayed in the breeze, the distant hum of conversations from the students leaving for the day. For a moment, she let herself feel the peace of simply existing, without the constant drumbeat of expectations.

As she walked home, her mind wandered back to the conversation in the restroom, to the tears she'd tried so hard to hide. She thought about the articles she'd read, the list of "stress management tips" that only seemed to make her feel more inadequate. And the words from Kunal's blog—Perfection is not a goal; it's a cycle. Maybe that was it. Maybe the endless pursuit of perfection wasn't something she could fix by just working harder, doing more, or pushing herself further. Maybe it was the pursuit itself that was the problem.

Her thoughts were interrupted when her phone buzzed in her pocket. For a moment, she hesitated. Part of her wanted to ignore it, to keep walking in this newfound space where the digital world didn't control her. But curiosity won. She pulled out the phone, unlocking it.

It was a message from Meera: "Sanya, I know you've been stressed, but just so you know, you're doing great. I see all the effort you put in. And I think you need a break—don't let the pressure eat you up. ♥?"

The words felt like a balm. Meera had no idea what Sanya had been going through, but somehow, she saw her.

The real Sanya. Not the version she presented on Instagram, not the girl who aced every test and looked flawless in every photo, but the person behind all that—a person who was tired, unsure, and struggling to find her way.

Sanya felt the knot in her chest loosen, just a little. Maybe I don't have to do this alone, she thought. Maybe I don't have to pretend anymore.

She typed back quickly, her fingers flying over the screen. "Thanks, Meera. I needed to hear that."

She paused for a moment, considering something. Then, with a deep breath, she added, "I've been feeling... a lot of pressure lately. It's exhausting, pretending I'm okay when I'm not. But I don't know how to stop."

The message hovered on the screen for a while, and Sanya almost deleted it. She'd never been this vulnerable before, at least not in such a direct way. But then, with a small sigh, she pressed send.

It didn't take long for Meera to reply. "You don't have to stop, Sanya. Just take a break. You're allowed to be human. And I'm here for you. Whenever."

Sanya smiled as she read the message, a quiet warmth spreading through her. The world hadn't ended because she admitted she wasn't perfect. In fact, it felt... freeing.

She continued her walk home, the weight lifting even more with every step. When she reached her front door, she was met with the usual greeting from her mother—warm, comforting, but as usual, expectant.

"Hi, darling! How was your day?" her mom asked, as she pulled her into a hug.

Sanya hugged her back, letting herself relax for the first time that day. "It was... okay," she said softly. "Just tired, you know?"

Her mom pulled back slightly, her expression gentle. "I know. You're doing so much, sweetie. You're amazing."

The words felt different now. Less like an expectation and more like love. Sanya could feel the difference. She wasn't trying to live up to anything in this moment. She was just her—tired, imperfect, but loved nonetheless.

After dinner, Sanya went to her room, a little quieter than usual, but also a little more peaceful. The weight of the world didn't feel so heavy. As she sat at her desk, her eyes glanced at her phone again, but this time, the urge to check it didn't control her. She didn't care about how many likes her latest post had gotten. She didn't care about the notifications she had missed. She cared about this—the stillness, the silence, the moment of peace that existed beyond the digital noise.

She took a deep breath and opened a new document on her laptop. Instead of scrolling through social media or obsessing over schoolwork, she began typing. Slowly at first, unsure of what would come, but then with more confidence as the words flowed. She wrote about her day, about the pressure she had been feeling, about the mask she had worn for so long.

It wasn't a perfect narrative. There were typos, fragments, and unfinished thoughts. But it was real. For the first time in ages, she wrote about herself—not the version that everyone else saw, but the one who was struggling, the one who felt trapped in the cycle of perfection. It was messy, it was raw, and it felt liberating.

As she closed her laptop for the night, Sanya felt a sense of clarity she hadn't felt in a long time. The pressure, the need to be perfect, hadn't disappeared, but it no longer held the same power over her. She had taken the first step, not toward perfection, but toward acceptance. Of herself. Of her imperfections. Of the fact that she didn't have to be flawless to be worthy of love, friendship, or success.

And as she lay in bed that night, she realized something important: She was enough. Not because of her grades, or the way she looked, or the number of likes she got. But because, despite everything, she was still standing, still moving forward. Even if it was just one step at a time.

The journey wasn't over, and it wouldn't be easy. But Sanya was ready. Ready to take the mask off. Ready to face herself—flaws, fears, and all. Because, in the end, the only perfection she needed was the kind that allowed her to be her true self. And that, she realized, was more than enough.

As sleep finally began to pull her under, Sanya smiled softly. The weight was still there, but it was lighter now. And for the first time in a long time, she let herself drift into a peaceful sleep, knowing she didn't have to be perfect to be whole.

The next morning, Sanya woke up with a sense of quiet resolve. The sun was filtering through her curtains, casting soft, warm rays across her room. It wasn't the frantic rush she usually felt when waking up to an overflowing to-do list. No, today felt different—calmer, gentler, as though the world was giving her a little bit of space to breathe.

She stretched, then checked her phone, half-expecting to feel that familiar anxiety when faced with the endless notifications. But this time, there was something else: a message from Meera.

"Morning! I've been thinking... We should talk more about this, like really talk. You don't have to go through this alone."

Sanya smiled at the message. It was simple, but it felt like a lifeline. Meera wasn't trying to fix her, wasn't asking her to be perfect. She was just offering to be there. For the first time, Sanya realized she didn't have to navigate this journey in isolation. There were people who cared about her—not for her grades, or her image, but for her.

Sanya typed a reply: "I'd like that. I think it's time to stop pretending. I'll talk to you soon."

She felt the weight lift a little more with every word she typed, and when she put the phone down, there was a lightness in her chest. She wasn't sure where this path would lead, but for once, it didn't feel like a never-ending maze of obligations and expectations. It felt like a choice, a choice to walk through life without the mask.

The day went on as it usually did—school, assignments, lunch with friends—but there was a new undercurrent to everything. When she sat in class, she didn't feel the usual pressure to perform. She answered questions when she felt confident, and when she didn't, she let herself sit in quiet contemplation instead of panicking about every detail. It felt... free.

Even in the lunchroom, she wasn't as concerned with how she looked, or whether her Instagram feed would reflect her best self. She laughed with Meera and the others, but this time, she didn't hide behind a smile. She let her emotions show, even when it wasn't always "comfortable."

Later, when the school bell rang and the final class was dismissed, Sanya wasn't in a hurry to leave. She took a moment to step outside, standing near the school gates, watching the students disperse in all directions. She felt the shift in herself—a quiet change, something she couldn't quite articulate, but something she could feel.

Her phone buzzed again. It was a reminder from her mom: "Don't forget to eat something healthy tonight. We love you!" The reminder felt different today. It wasn't just an obligation; it was a reminder that someone cared for her, that even the smallest things mattered. And the love behind it? It made everything seem just a little bit easier to handle.

Sanya didn't rush home today. Instead, she made her way to a local café that she loved, one that had a small but comforting atmosphere. She sat down by the window, ordered a cup of tea, and let her thoughts wander.

She thought about everything that had happened in the last 24 hours—the bathroom stall, the message from Meera, the quiet realization that she was enough as she was. It was strange, this freedom she was starting to feel. She didn't have all the answers, didn't have it all figured out, but she was finally allowing herself to be.

As she sipped her tea, her mind drifted to the upcoming weekend. Meera had invited her to the hangout with their friends. Usually, Sanya would've said yes out of obligation, eager to fit in and keep up the façade. But this time, something inside her hesitated. Was it because she didn't feel like going? Or because she was afraid of letting go of the image of the perfect student, the perfect friend?

Maybe it was both. But that's when it clicked—maybe it wasn't about saying yes to everything just to keep up appearances. Maybe it was about giving herself the space to choose. To decide what she wanted, without fear of disappointing anyone.

Sanya pulled out her phone and quickly sent a message to Meera: "Hey, I've been thinking. I think I'll skip the hangout this time. I need some time for myself, to just unwind."

She waited, a slight flutter in her chest as she hit send. But when Meera replied, it was with complete understanding: "Totally get it. Take care of yourself, okay? We'll catch up soon."

It felt good to know she wasn't letting anyone down by choosing her own peace. Sanya finished her tea and sat there for a while, lost in the quiet rhythm of her own thoughts. She realized that, for the first time in a long time, she wasn't looking for validation from the outside world. She was starting to find it within herself.

Later that evening, as she sat down with her homework, she noticed something. The anxiety she had usually felt about her assignments wasn't there, or at least not in the same overwhelming way. She was focused, yes, but it wasn't a frantic, pressure-filled focus. It was more... calm. She didn't have to prove anything. She could just do her work at her own pace, without the panic or need to be perfect.

When she finished, she didn't immediately turn to social media for a distraction. Instead, she took a walk outside, letting the cool evening air clear her mind. The stars had just begun to appear in the sky, and Sanya found herself standing still, looking up at the vastness of it all. She felt small in comparison, but not insignificant. It was the opposite—she felt part of something much larger, a world full of people who, like her, were trying to figure things out, trying to find their place.

As she walked back into her house, a thought crossed her mind: I'm allowed to be imperfect. I'm allowed to have bad days, to struggle, to not have everything under control. And that's okay.

For the first time, she truly believed it.

She was a warrior, not because she could do it all, but because she was willing to face each day, each challenge, with courage and honesty. She didn't need to hide anymore. She didn't need to be perfect.

The journey ahead wasn't going to be easy. There would be moments of doubt, moments when the weight of the world would press on her again. But for now, Sanya knew something deep inside her had shifted. The battle wasn't about perfection. It was about finding the strength to be herself, to accept her flaws, and to trust that, in time, she would find her way.

And that was more than enough.

VI

The Teenage Warrior - Reflection

Perfectionism is the belief that you must be flawless in every aspect of your life. It often manifests as the constant pursuit of unrealistic, unattainable standards—whether in academics, appearance, relationships, or personal achievements. The pressure to "be perfect" can come from various sources: societal expectations, family pressures, social media comparisons, and even internal desires to feel in control and accomplished.

However, what many don't realize is that perfectionism isn't about striving for the best version of ourselves—it's about trying to avoid failure, rejection, or disappointment at all costs. It's a constant attempt to meet a version of "success" that society has created, a version that doesn't leave room for human error or vulnerability.

While striving for excellence can be motivating, perfectionism often leads to self-criticism, anxiety, and feelings of inadequacy. It can make you feel like you're never good enough, no matter how hard you try, which can take a toll on your mental and emotional well-being.

In Sanya's story, perfectionism is seen in the way she feels the weight of every test score, every social interaction, and every post on social media. She internalizes the idea that if she doesn't live up to these pressures, she's somehow failing, even though no one else is asking her to be perfect. This constant pressure, although initially motivated by ambition, soon becomes a burden, leading her to feel overwhelmed, exhausted, and disconnected from her true self.

Perfectionism often prevents us from embracing the idea that mistakes are part of growth. It sets us up for failure by making us believe that unless we are flawless, we're not worthy. It turns every setback into a reason to judge ourselves harshly, and every success into an opportunity to push even harder, without ever allowing ourselves to relax or celebrate.

In the long run, it can cause burnout. The constant striving to be "perfect" can strip away your sense of satisfaction and make you feel like you're never enough, leading to chronic stress, anxiety, and even depression.

It also isolates you. When you're constantly putting on the mask of perfection, you're not giving people the chance to truly get to know you. You're too busy keeping up appearances, hiding the flaws and fears that everyone else feels, too. In doing so, we risk losing genuine connections with others and even with ourselves.

Breaking the Cycle of Perfectionism

Recognize the signs: Understanding when perfectionism is affecting us is the first step. If we find ourselves constantly feeling overwhelmed, stressed, or inadequate, it's time to reevaluate our expectations.

Be kind to yourself: Perfectionism thrives in environments of self-criticism. If you can learn to show yourself the same kindness you would show a friend, it can ease the internal pressure.

Set realistic goals: It's important to set achievable goals for yourself and recognize that mistakes are part of the learning process.

Build a support system: Surround yourself with people who accept you for who you are, not for what you achieve. This allows room for vulnerability and authenticity, which are essential for mental health.

Find value in progress, not perfection: Celebrate the steps you take, even the small ones. Progress is progress, no matter how slow.

As the story of Sanya unfolded, we saw how her journey through the pressures of perfectionism gradually led to a quieter, more peaceful existence. She wasn't magically free from the burdens she carried, but she started to see that they didn't define her. She was not her grades, her social media image, or the expectations others had for her. She was more than that. Sanya learned that she didn't have to sacrifice her mental health or her true self to meet the standards that others placed on her. The journey toward accepting imperfection is never a straight line, and Sanya's path, while not free of setbacks, was filled with small steps of self-acceptance.

In the process, Sanya discovered that real strength comes from knowing who you are, flaws and all, and being unapologetically true to that version of yourself. We live in a world that often values achievements and appearances more than authenticity, but at the end of the day, the only standard we need to meet is our own.

Dear Friend,

If you're reading this, I want you to know that I see you. I know what it feels like to carry the weight of the world on your shoulders, to constantly feel like you have to be perfect at everything. Maybe you're trying to be the best student, the perfect friend, or the flawless version of yourself online. I get it. I've been there, too.

For so long, I thought that if I could just get it right—whether it was acing every test, fitting into a certain mold, or always having my life together—then maybe I'd finally be enough. But here's the truth I had to learn the hard way: Perfection is a lie.

Perfectionism isn't about being the best—it's about never letting yourself be anything less than what you think the world expects. And when you can't meet those impossible standards, you feel like a failure. I've felt that too—the panic, the anxiety, the pressure. It's exhausting. It wears you down in ways you don't even realize.

But here's something that changed everything for me: I realized I didn't have to be perfect to be valuable. It was okay to not have all the answers. It was okay to make mistakes. It was okay to be imperfect. And I could still be worthy of love and respect, even when I wasn't at my best.

I know it's hard to believe that sometimes, especially when social media, school, and even family pressures make you feel like you're falling short. But I'm here to tell you that you are enough—just as you are. You don't have to be perfect to be worthy. You don't have to have it all figured out. You don't have to pretend to be okay when you're not.

I used to think that if I showed vulnerability or admitted that I was struggling, it meant I was weak. But the truth is, being vulnerable takes incredible strength. It means you're willing to let go of the mask you wear and show the world who you really are, flaws and all. And that's more than enough.

If you're like me, you've probably spent a lot of time trying to meet everyone else's expectations. But I want you to know that it's okay to let go of that. It's okay to say no when you're too tired, to take a step back when the world feels too overwhelming, and to put yourself first. Your mental health, your peace, and your happiness matter more than any test score, social media post, or achievement.

I'm still learning how to live this way every day. There are moments when the pressure sneaks back in, and I feel the weight of the world again. But I've learned that the key isn't to be perfect—it's to be real, to be kind to myself, and to trust that I'm enough, no matter what.

So if you're struggling with perfectionism, know this: You don't have to carry that weight alone. It's okay to ask for help. It's okay to take breaks. And most importantly, it's okay to not be perfect. The world is full of people just like you—people who are learning to embrace their imperfections and who are growing stronger every day by doing so.

Take a deep breath, let go of the pressure, and remember that you are already enough. You don't need to do anything more than show up as yourself.

With all my love and support,
Sanya

VII
Caregiver on Empty

Mira had always been the kind of girl who felt like she had to do it all. From the time she could remember, she was the one organizing the family events, making sure her younger brother's shoes were on the right feet, packing her mom's lunch before work. She was a planner, a doer. There was never a task too big or too small that Mira didn't take head-on. But somehow, no one had ever taught her how to take care of herself.

It wasn't as if she didn't try. Every few months, her friends would talk about the latest self-care trends: face masks, bubble baths, "me-time" journaling. Mira would nod along, but in the back of her mind, she was already wondering, When do I have time for that?

When her father got sick, the word "self-care" slipped away like an old habit, something she couldn't quite remember how to do anymore. The transition wasn't dramatic at first. There was no big bang, no warning bell —

just a slow, creeping shift. Her father had been ill for years, sure, but not this sick. Not the kind of sick that consumed your thoughts, your time, your every waking moment.

The first time she saw him collapse, she'd been too stunned to think. One moment, he was sitting at the dining table, talking about his day, sipping his tea like it was any other evening. The next, he was on the floor, face pale, barely breathing. It was as though the life had been sucked out of him, and Mira, in that moment, felt her whole world shift beneath her feet.

She remembered calling for her mother, who ran in, frantic, then the ambulance, the hospital, the doctors who spoke in sterile, emotionless tones. "Stage three lymphoma." The words clung to the air, suffocating. Her mind couldn't quite process them, but they kept coming back: "Stage three."

That night, when her mom came home after staying at the hospital, Mira didn't know what to do. She should've comforted her mother, told her it would be okay. But how could she? There was no "okay" anymore. There was only the reality of what was happening to the person who had always been strong, steady, her father, the man who had always taken care of her. Now, it was up to Mira.

Weeks turned into months, and everything became a blur. She didn't notice the days slipping by or the weight of responsibility piling on her shoulders. At first, it was small things: setting alarms for his medications, picking up prescriptions, staying up late researching the best treatments, attending doctor's appointments, and tracking his symptoms. These were just the new routines of her life.

She would get up in the morning, make breakfast for her father, help him to the couch where he would spend the day resting, and then she'd go to school, trying to act normal.

But school felt like an empty shell. Her friends noticed, but no one asked.

At lunch, they chatted about prom plans and who was dating who, oblivious to the chaos she was holding together with the smallest threads. Mira wasn't good at asking for help. That wasn't her thing. Besides, she had this. She always had everything under control, didn't she? The A+ student, the responsible one, the girl with the endless energy and unshakable optimism. That's how people saw her, even as the cracks started to form under the surface.

She stopped sleeping. It started as just a few hours here and there, but soon it stretched to a full week of two or three hours a night. She started getting tired in class, nodding off during history lectures, her mind constantly buzzing with thoughts of medications, meals, laundry, and the million little tasks she had to remember. But no one noticed. Or, if they did, they didn't care to ask. They couldn't see how empty she felt, how much of herself she had already given away.

Her friends still texted, but the messages felt distant, like postcards from a life she could no longer reach. "How's everything?" one of them asked. Mira would reply with the same rehearsed answer, "Fine, busy. Just a lot going on." But she wasn't fine. She wasn't even close.

When she came home after school, she'd spend an hour or two fixing dinner — for herself, for her father, for her mom when she'd come home exhausted from work. She'd leave the kitchen late at night, scrubbed clean, but her body felt heavier with each passing day. She hadn't gone out with friends in months. Not for prom dress shopping. Not for movies. Not for a single fun thing. Her world was now a never-ending loop of caregiving.

One night, her father couldn't even get out of bed. She had to carry him to the bathroom. He was weak, his body frail, and she could feel his ribs against her hands, like she was holding on to something about to shatter. As she helped him back to bed, he looked up at her, his tired eyes filled with gratitude, but she saw something else there too — an apology. His gaze seemed to say, I'm sorry you're carrying this for me.

The guilt hit her like a tidal wave.

She couldn't stop the tears. They fell silently, one after another, while she held her father's hand. For the first time, Mira felt like the weight of the world was too much. But she didn't say anything. What would she even say? Who could she tell? There was no one else. She was the one who had to carry it.

It wasn't long after that night that Mira noticed her body starting to fall apart in ways she couldn't ignore anymore. Her legs ached constantly, her back throbbed from hours spent hunched over helping her father, and she started getting sharp headaches. But what could she do? Stop? Quit? She wasn't allowed to. Not when he needed her.

One afternoon, after giving her father his medication, she sat in the kitchen, staring at the kettle on the stove. It had been whistling for a while, but she hadn't noticed. The sound had become part of the background noise of her life, like the constant ringing in her ears that she hadn't been able to silence for weeks.

Mira reached for the kettle, not even realizing her hands were shaking until she touched it. It was empty. The boiling sound, high-pitched and frantic, echoed in the room, as if mocking her. Empty. Just like she felt. She stared at the kettle for a long time, the steam rising in the air, and she understood for the first time in weeks — she couldn't keep doing this alone.

Her body was running on fumes, and her mind was a maze of exhaustion. She wasn't just tired. She was burned out. She had given everything she had, but the more she gave, the more the world seemed to take.

She sat down, feeling as if the floor beneath her had cracked wide open. It wasn't a dramatic breakdown. It wasn't a sobbing, messy collapse. It was quieter than that, a hollow realization, a slow sinking feeling that she hadn't just been pouring herself out — she had been vanishing.

"You can't pour from an empty kettle," she whispered to herself, a phrase she had read in an article once. It had never made sense before, but now it did. She had been running on empty for so long that she hadn't even known how close she was to breaking.

And for the first time in months, Mira didn't know what to do. She felt lost. And that was a feeling she couldn't fix with a to-do list.

Mira sat there for a long time, staring at the kettle, the silence filling up the space like thick fog. Her father, in the next room, was quiet too — no coughing, no calls for help. Just the sound of his shallow breaths, punctuated by the distant hum of the refrigerator. It was as if everything had come to a standstill, waiting for her to do something. But what? What was there left to do when it felt like you were already doing everything?

She let the tears slip down her face. They came slowly, unbidden, like water from a cracked dam that had been holding back the flood. For so long, she had been the rock — the one who kept it all together. But what if she couldn't be strong anymore? What if she wasn't strong at all?

Her thoughts spiraled into confusion. She had always been proud of her ability to manage everything, to juggle responsibilities like a circus performer balancing spinning plates. But now, as she looked at the empty kettle, the truth settled in her chest like a weight: She had no more plates to spin. And if she didn't figure out how to stop, she was going to fall.

The kettle's whistling sound had stopped, but the ringing in her ears hadn't. It was a reminder, a call she couldn't ignore anymore. Mira stood up slowly, her legs unsteady as if she had forgotten how to walk. She didn't know what to do with herself. Should she cry? Scream? Run? But instead, she did the hardest thing of all: she called someone.

Her phone felt heavy in her hand, like a lifeline, but also like a burden. The list of people she could call seemed empty — her mom was at work, her friends were busy with their own lives. Who could she possibly ask for help? Who could understand what she was going through?

Mira thought of her aunt, Aarti, her mother's younger sister, who had always been a source of comfort. She picked up her phone and hesitated for just a moment, then pressed call.

It rang twice before Aarti's voice picked up, warm and familiar. "Mira? Is everything okay?"

Mira's throat tightened, but she managed to speak. "Aunt Aarti... I don't know what to do. I need help. I don't know what to do anymore."

There was a brief silence on the other end. Aarti's voice softened. "Sweetheart, I know it's hard. I know you've been holding so much. But you don't have to do this alone. You are not alone."

The words landed in Mira's chest like a gentle breeze, not a harsh wind. You are not alone. It was the first time anyone had said it — not her father, not her mother, not her friends. They were too busy thinking of her as the pillar holding everything up, to realize she was cracking at the seams.

"I don't know how to stop," Mira admitted. "I don't know how to take a break. Every time I try, I feel like I'm failing him. Like I'm abandoning him."

Aarti sighed softly, understanding in her tone. "You're not abandoning him, Mira. Taking care of yourself isn't abandoning anyone. It's the only way you can keep going. You can't pour from an empty kettle."

The phrase from earlier echoed in her mind. Mira felt like she was starting to understand it, slowly, piece by piece. She had been running on fumes for so long, trying to take care of her father without taking care of herself. But that wasn't sustainable. It wasn't healthy. And no matter how much she wished she could do it all, she couldn't.

Aarti continued. "You need rest, Mira. You need to lean on the people around you. Your dad needs you, yes, but he needs you healthy too. You don't have to be everything for everyone. You just have to show up when you can — and when you can't, it's okay to ask for help."

For the first time in what felt like forever, Mira felt something inside her relax — a tension she didn't even know she had been holding. She could breathe again. And in that breath, she realized something important: it wasn't a sign of weakness to ask for help. It was a sign of strength.

The next day, she didn't go to school. She called in sick, and for the first time, it felt like the most responsible decision she had made in a long time. She spent the morning lying in bed, not doing anything. At first, it felt foreign, uncomfortable — like she was betraying the routine she had built. But as the hours passed, she began to feel something shift inside her. She wasn't being lazy. She was healing.

Her phone buzzed. It was Aarti, asking if she needed anything. "I'm okay," Mira texted back. "Just... resting."

Mira didn't know what the future would hold, or how long her father's battle would last. But she knew one thing: She was not invincible. She couldn't keep doing everything alone. And asking for help didn't mean she was failing. It meant she was taking the first step to saving herself so she could continue caring for those she loved.

That night, she sat by her father's bedside, holding his hand as she always did. But this time, she didn't feel like she was drowning. She didn't feel like the weight of the world was crushing her. She felt... okay. It wasn't a perfect moment, but it was enough.

For the first time in a long time, Mira realized that she was worthy of care — just as much as anyone else. And maybe, just maybe, that would be the beginning of her healing too.

The following days were a blur. But a different kind of blur — one that didn't make Mira feel like she was sinking. The exhaustion still lingered, but it wasn't as crushing anymore. She had begun to accept that she couldn't do everything. And with that acceptance, something unexpected happened: she didn't have to.

Her aunt, Aarti, kept calling, checking in, offering help. "I can come over this weekend," she'd said, "and help with some of the chores around the house. You don't need to do everything yourself."

Mira hesitated at first. She didn't want to feel like she was burdening anyone. But she knew deep down that Aarti wasn't offering out of obligation — she genuinely wanted to help. She wanted Mira to take a breath, to rest, to reclaim some of the pieces of herself that had been lost in the chaos.

The weekend came, and Aarti showed up, not just to help with the chores, but to spend time with her. They didn't talk about her father's illness. Instead, they baked together. Aarti brought a recipe from their childhood — coconut ladoos, soft and fragrant with cardamom. For the first time in a long time, Mira found herself laughing, the sound coming from somewhere deep within her that she hadn't heard in months. The weight wasn't gone, but it was lighter. And she was learning how to live alongside it, instead of letting it define her.

That Saturday evening, Mira took her first real nap in weeks. She slept for three hours straight, completely unaware of the time passing, and woke up feeling something she had long forgotten — rested.

But even with the small changes, it wasn't all easy. Mira still had moments when the pressure felt too much. When she'd look at her father and see the hollow eyes, the way his skin had thinned, her heart would break. She would feel the familiar knot in her chest, the instinct to care for him first and herself second. Old habits died hard.

There were days when she'd forget to eat, or skip a shower because she felt like she didn't have the time. And on those days, the guilt would come rushing in. But now, instead of pushing it away, Mira let it sit with her. She would acknowledge it, name it, and then, when it got too loud, she'd speak out loud to herself: "It's okay. I can't do it all. And asking for help doesn't make me weak. It makes me human."

Her friends, too, began to notice the changes. It wasn't a huge, sweeping shift. It wasn't like Mira suddenly turned into someone who could juggle everything with perfect ease. But when they asked how she was doing, she didn't lie. She didn't say she was fine anymore. Instead, she would say,

"It's hard, but I'm doing the best I can. I'm learning how to take care of myself, too."

It was an uncomfortable honesty, but it felt like a freedom she had never experienced before.

The real turning point came a few weeks later when Mira sat with her father one evening, watching him slowly sip the cup of tea she'd made for him. He had been quiet, his gaze distant, as he so often was these days, but that night, he looked at her. Really looked at her, his tired eyes softening, like he was seeing her for the first time in ages.

"Mira," he said, his voice weak but clear. "You've been doing so much. Too much. I... I don't know how to ask this, but... are you okay?"

The words hit her like a wave. She hadn't expected him to notice. She hadn't thought that he, in his own battle, would recognize the weight she had been carrying. For so long, she had been the one caring for him, helping him hold it together. But now, she realized that he had been holding her together, too, even in his silence. He had seen her struggle, and he wanted to know if she was okay.

Mira paused, feeling the sting of vulnerability in her chest. She wanted to say yes, that everything was fine. But instead, she answered truthfully, "No, Dad. I'm not okay. But I'm working on it. I'm learning how to ask for help. I'm learning how to take care of myself, too."

Her father's hand reached out, weak but steady, and he took hers. "I'm proud of you," he whispered. "You don't have to be perfect, Mira. You're doing your best. That's all anyone can ask of you."

And in that moment, a weight she hadn't even known she was carrying lifted. Mira realized that her father, despite everything, still saw her. He still saw her — not just as his caregiver, but as his daughter. And that was enough.

The next few weeks were a mix of continued caregiving and new habits. Mira began setting boundaries, small ones at first. She asked for help when she needed it. She took naps, went on short walks, and even rejoined a few study sessions with her friends. It wasn't easy — old patterns die hard — but she was learning, day by day, how to take care of herself without feeling guilty.

And she knew, deep down, that her father, though he still needed her, was also proud of the woman she was becoming. He wanted her to be healthy, to live her life, not just exist in the shadow of his illness.

Mira wasn't perfect. She wasn't a superhero. But for the first time in a long time, she was enough. And she could live with that.

It had been a few months since Mira had started to take small steps towards caring for herself. The weight of caregiving was still present, of course, but it wasn't all-consuming anymore. It was like carrying a heavy bag — but now, she had learned how to adjust the straps so it didn't dig into her shoulders as painfully. Sometimes, she still felt the sharpness of fatigue, the temptation to slip back into her old habits. But now, she recognized it for what it was: an old pattern, one she didn't have to follow.

One afternoon, as she sat with her father in the living room, her phone buzzed with a message from her best friend, Aria.

"Hey! You up for a movie night tonight? I know things have been crazy for you lately. You deserve a break, Mira."

Mira hesitated. A movie night? It sounded... nice. Too nice. She glanced at her father, who was dozing lightly on the couch next to her. She had been his constant, his everything, for so long that the idea of stepping away for even a few hours felt almost wrong. But then, something inside her shifted. She wasn't betraying her father by taking a night off. He wasn't an anchor that kept her tied to one place — he was a part of her life, but so was she. And she needed this.

She quickly typed back.

"I'm in. I'll be there in two hours."

The excitement in her chest surprised her. It had been so long since she had done something just for herself — something that wasn't tied to her father's needs. She made a mental note to check in with him before she left, to make sure he had everything he needed for the evening. Then, she took a deep breath and stood up, feeling the rare rush of anticipation in her veins.

That evening, Mira found herself sitting on Aria's couch, a bowl of popcorn between them, watching some lighthearted rom-com. It felt like she had stepped into another world — a world where the only thing that mattered was the laughter that filled the room. For the first time in what felt like forever, Mira let herself just be. No caregiving. No responsibilities. No expectations. Just a night to unwind and be with a friend.

Aria glanced at her. "You know, Mira, I've been meaning to ask — how are you, really? You've been a little distant lately. I get it, with everything going on with your dad, but I just want to make sure you're okay."

Mira looked at her friend, surprised at how seen she felt in that moment. There was no judgment, no pity — just genuine care. "I'm getting there," she said, her voice softer than she expected. "I've been... working on it. Learning to take care of myself, too. It's been a lot. But tonight feels good. It feels like I'm actually... living again."

Aria smiled. "I'm glad to hear that. You deserve to live, Mira. Not just survive."

It was a simple statement, but it hit Mira hard. Living. That's what she had forgotten to do for so long. She hadn't been living; she had been treading water, holding on so tightly to everything and everyone around her, thinking that if she just kept holding on, everything would stay afloat. But now, she was starting to see that in order to truly stay afloat, she had to let go a little. She had to let herself breathe.

The next few days were marked by this new awareness. Mira still cared for her father with the same dedication, but there was a difference now. She wasn't running on empty anymore. She was taking breaks when she needed them, stepping away when it was time to recharge. She would take short walks in the evenings, listen to music while cooking dinner, or spend an hour curled up with a book — all things that felt like small acts of rebellion against the person she had been before.

She also found herself reaching out more — not just for help, but for connection. Her old habits of isolation were starting to fade. She began calling Aarti more often, sharing bits of her day and asking for advice when she needed it. She reached out to her friends, even when it felt like the last thing she had the energy for. It was hard, but it was also freeing.

One Saturday, as Mira was tidying up the house, her father called her into the living room. His voice sounded weak, but there was something different in it — a softness, a gentleness that made Mira pause.

"Mira," he said, his hands shaking slightly as he motioned for her to sit next to him. "I need to tell you something."

Her heart skipped. Was it bad news? She sat down, her mind racing.

"You've been amazing," he continued, his voice quiet but firm. "But I want you to know, it's okay to let go sometimes. You don't have to carry it all. I've seen how much you've been giving. And I want you to know that it's enough. I'm proud of you."

Mira felt tears welling up in her eyes. This wasn't the first time her father had expressed gratitude for her, but there was something different in his tone now. It was as if he truly understood the burden she had been carrying — and was telling her, with every fiber of his being, that it was okay to step back. That it was okay to let herself have a life.

For the first time in a long while, Mira allowed herself to cry — not out of exhaustion or frustration, but out of relief. She wasn't alone in this. She didn't have to do it all. And even if the road ahead was still difficult, she had permission — from her father, from Aarti, from herself — to take care of her own heart, too.

That evening, Mira sat by her father's side, holding his hand just as she always did. But this time, the silence between them wasn't heavy. It wasn't a silence filled with unsaid things or unspoken burdens. It was a silence filled with understanding. And in that quiet, Mira realized something that changed everything: she had been giving her heart away for so long, but now, she was learning how to keep some of it for herself. And that made all the difference.

The weeks that followed were still challenging, but they were different. Mira had learned to adjust the rhythm of her life — to give herself space without feeling guilty, to ask for help without feeling weak. She still spent the majority of her days caring for her father, but now, those days didn't feel like a never-ending cycle of sacrifice. There was a balance that felt like a gift, a quiet revelation that she didn't have to lose herself in the process of loving someone else.

One morning, after breakfast, her father turned to her with a soft smile, his eyes no longer as clouded by illness. He had his moments of weakness, of course — there were good days and bad days — but lately, he had seemed lighter. Calmer. And it wasn't just because of the medication. It was because he had accepted his limitations, and in doing so, had given Mira permission to live her own life as well.

"Mira," he began, his voice still raspy, but the words filled with warmth. "I've been thinking. You're young, you're strong, and you deserve to have a life of your own. I don't want you to sacrifice everything for me. You're not just my caregiver; you're my daughter. And you deserve to be happy."

Mira's breath caught in her throat. It wasn't the first time her father had said something like this, but today, it felt different. Today, she heard it not as an obligation, but as a love that had no strings attached.

She felt tears welling up again, but this time they were different. They weren't born from frustration or sadness; they were born from the overwhelming sense of being seen. Really seen. By the one person who had been her anchor for so long.

"I... I don't know what to say," she whispered, her voice thick. "But I'll try. I'll try to live, Dad. I promise."

For a moment, the two of them just sat there in quiet understanding, each acknowledging the other's struggles and triumphs. Mira didn't know how much longer her father would need her, or how much longer they would have together. But in that moment, she realized that it didn't matter. She could live, and she could love him, and it would be enough.

The following month, Mira made the decision to take a week off from caregiving — a real, honest-to-goodness break. It wasn't easy at first; the guilt crept in, as it always did. But she told herself that she was doing this for both of them. She booked a trip to a nearby hill station with Aria, something she had wanted to do for years but had never allowed herself to. She needed this — a space to be herself, without the weight of responsibility.

The trip was simple but profound. She spent the week hiking, reading by a quiet lake, and reconnecting with herself in a way that felt like a rebirth. She didn't have to be anyone else's hero. She didn't have to be perfect. She was just Mira, a young woman who had been through a lot, and who had learned the importance of taking care of herself.

When she came back, she felt different. Lighter. She had new energy, a renewed sense of purpose. And when she returned home to her father, she didn't feel drained. She felt present. She had found a way to be there for him while also being there for herself.

One evening, months later, as Mira sat on the porch with her father, watching the sunset, she realized something. She had stopped running. She had stopped trying to do everything at once, stopped believing that her worth was tied to how much she could give. She had learned that self-care wasn't selfish — it was essential. And that was something no one could take away from her.

Her father, once a source of so much pain and worry, was now a reminder of the importance of both love and limits. The struggle they had faced had taught them both something vital — that life was not just about surviving, but about learning how to live fully, with balance, with grace.

As they sat together in silence, the warmth of the fading sun casting a golden glow on their faces, Mira felt a quiet pride in herself. She had done the impossible: she had learned to care for someone else without losing herself. And in doing so, she had discovered a power inside her that she never knew existed.

And now, she was ready to face whatever came next — with strength, with love, and with the understanding that she, too, deserved to live.

VIII

Caregiver on Empty - Reflection

Caregiving refers to the act of providing assistance and support to individuals who are unable to care for themselves due to illness, aging, or disability. This role often falls to family members, especially daughters and spouses, and can be both physically and emotionally demanding. It may involve tasks such as administering medication, helping with daily activities, and providing emotional support. Caregiving can become an invisible, often overwhelming labor, especially when the needs of the caregiver themselves go unmet.

Self-care is the practice of taking an active role in protecting one's own well-being and happiness, particularly during times of stress. This includes activities that nurture the body, mind, and soul. Self-care can range from physical activities like exercise and sleep to emotional practices like journaling, meditation, or spending time with loved ones. It's not a luxury — it's an essential part of sustaining overall health and ensuring that we have the energy to care for others without burning out.

Boundaries are the limits we set with others regarding what is acceptable and unacceptable behavior. In the context of caregiving, it involves communicating and maintaining healthy limits on what you can and cannot do for others. Boundaries help protect your time, energy, and emotional well-being, ensuring that you are not overwhelmed or taken for granted.

Mira's story, while deeply personal, is also a reflection of a broader issue that many women, especially caregivers, face. The culture of self-sacrifice and invisible labor has been ingrained in many societies for generations. Women, particularly daughters and wives, are often expected to prioritize the needs of others over their own. This can lead to a dangerous cycle of burnout, exhaustion, and emotional depletion. But there's something vital that we must understand: self-care isn't selfish.

Caregiving — whether it's for a parent, a partner, or a child — often goes unnoticed, and its emotional and physical toll is seldom acknowledged. In Mira's case, she took on the role of her father's primary caregiver, which meant managing his health, his needs, and everything that came with his illness. Yet, she was expected to give without any recognition of her own struggles.

Invisible caregiving is a hidden burden. It can be mentally and physically exhausting, and it often leaves little room for personal rest or recovery. The truth is that caregiving, though a noble role, can become toxic if not balanced with self-care. Mira's journey reflects the difficulty of understanding that taking care of yourself is essential to continue caring for others effectively.

Boundaries are often seen as rigid and impolite, especially in cultures where familial duty is held above individual needs. However, setting healthy boundaries is necessary for mental and emotional survival. Mira's story shows that setting boundaries doesn't mean abandoning your responsibilities — it means understanding your limitations and communicating them openly.

When Mira learned to say "no" to certain demands, or when she allowed herself to take time away from caregiving, it wasn't an act of neglect. It was an act of preserving her mental health and ensuring she could show up fully for her father, her friends, and herself.

Another crucial lesson from Mira's story is the importance of reaching out for support. For a long time, she felt the weight of her father's illness was hers alone to carry. But the turning point came when she accepted help from Aarti and her friends. Asking for help isn't a sign of weakness. It's a way of recognizing your own humanity and the fact that no one can do everything alone. It's okay to lean on others, to share your burdens, and to trust that your community wants to help.

Mira's journey is also about reclaiming the parts of herself that were lost. She started small: taking walks, having a movie night with friends, and gradually reintroducing small pleasures into her life. These small acts of self-care are not selfish. They are vital. When we allow ourselves space to breathe, to rest, and to live beyond our roles as caregivers, we allow our souls to recharge. This space can take many forms, but it's essential for sustaining the love and energy we give to others.

One of the most powerful emotions Mira had to confront was guilt. Guilt for not doing enough, for taking time for herself, for asking for help. This is something many women face. But what Mira's journey teaches is that guilt can be reframed. It's okay to prioritize your own well-being, to take breaks, and to rest. In fact, these actions will help you serve others better in the long run. Guilt doesn't have to be a driver of behavior — it can be a signal to check in with yourself and adjust your actions for your own health and happiness.

Dear You,

I don't know your story, but I know your struggle. The quiet exhaustion that fills your bones, the weight that presses on your chest every time you try to breathe, the overwhelming sense of responsibility that makes you feel like you're carrying the world — or worse, like you're failing when you can't do it all. I've been there. And it's hard. It's so hard.

But here's what I want you to know — you are allowed to rest. You are allowed to say, "I need help." You are allowed to take time for yourself. And it doesn't make you selfish. It makes you human.

For too long, I thought that being a good daughter, a good caregiver, meant sacrificing my own needs. I thought that if I just kept giving, kept pushing through the exhaustion, I'd eventually be enough. But I learned the hard way that you can't pour from an empty cup. You can't keep giving when you're running on fumes.

So, I want you to know that it's okay to step back. It's okay to take a break. It's okay to tell the world, "I need to take care of me right now." Because when you take care of yourself, you're giving more to the world, not less. When you care for yourself, you have more to give to the ones you love. You can't be everything for everyone, and that's okay.

Don't wait until you're burned out like I did. Don't let the guilt of caring for someone else stop you from caring for yourself. Trust me, the world won't fall apart if you take a day to recharge. And if you ever feel like you're too tired, too overwhelmed, to keep going — just remember, you don't have to do it all alone. There are people who want to help. You are not a burden for needing help. You are not less because you ask for support.

You are doing the best you can. And that's enough. So take a deep breath. You deserve peace. You deserve joy. You deserve to live beyond the roles you play.

I'm sending you all the love and strength I've gathered in this journey. You are stronger than you realize, and you will find balance. One step at a time.

With all my heart,

Mira

Mira's story isn't just about caregiving; it's about reclaiming the self. It's about learning to care for others without losing yourself in the process. We live in a world that often asks women to give endlessly, to sacrifice their time and energy without question. But the truth is that in order to give your best, you must take care of your own needs. In order to care for others, you must first learn to care for yourself.

We are all, in some way, caregivers. We care for our families, our friends, our communities. But the key lesson from Mira's journey is that true strength comes from balance. You cannot be a good caregiver if you are drained, burnt out, and forgotten. It is only by setting boundaries, asking for help, and prioritizing your own well-being that you can continue to show up for those who need you most.

To all the caregivers out there — this is your reminder: you matter. Your needs matter. And taking care of yourself is just as important as taking care of others. You are worthy of rest, of joy, and of love. Don't let anyone, including yourself, tell you otherwise.

IX

The Office Heroine

The fluorescent lights in the 18th-floor ladies' restroom hum like a broken hymn. Anika stands in front of the mirror, clutching the edge of the sink like it's the only thing keeping her from unraveling. She's in her blazer—navy blue, tailored perfectly. Her hair is slicked back into a low bun, neat enough to mean business but soft enough to avoid being called "too aggressive." Her lipstick is muted mauve—boardroom appropriate.

She looks every inch the young professional. But inside, she's barely holding on.

It's 8:07 a.m. The office hasn't even filled up yet, but Anika is already on edge. Her inbox has 47 unread emails. Her calendar is blocked top to bottom. There's a meeting in twenty minutes with Mr. Rajan—the man who insists on calling her "beta" in front of clients and "ambitious" like it's a warning.

She checks her phone. No messages from her best friend, no "good luck" text from her mom. Just a message from her team:

"Don't forget the pitch deck. They're expecting numbers."

Her stomach twists. They are always expecting numbers. From her.

She's 25. Fresh out of a top-tier business school, promoted early, and leading a team of five. It sounds impressive on paper. In real life? It's lonely. Every room she walks into, she's the only woman. Every time she speaks, she second-guesses herself. Did I sound too unsure? Too sharp? Too soft?

Anika's work speaks for itself—clients love her, her reports are flawless, and she's led two major projects to success. But praise is rare. She's seen the way her male colleagues get treated. Same output, louder applause. Same errors, softer feedback. One of them once interrupted her mid-presentation, reworded her idea, and got a nod of approval from the director. She smiled politely while her insides screamed.

The real killer, though, is the constant, creeping fear that she doesn't belong.

Every time she achieves something, a voice in her head whispers, "You just got lucky."
Every time someone praises her, it echoes, "They don't see the real you—the one who's just faking it."

It's imposter syndrome, textbook-style—but lived in color.

And no one talks about it. Not in quarterly reviews. Not in company retreats. Not over casual coffee machine gossip. It's a silent, private war.

Anika wages it alone.

The unspoken rules of the corporate jungle are brutal for women. Anika has learned them the hard way.

Rule #1: Smile. But not too much—they'll think you're unserious.
Rule #2: Speak up. But don't interrupt, even when you're

being interrupted.

Rule #3: Be confident. But be likable. No one likes a know-it-all.

Rule #4: Be grateful. Always. As if you didn't earn this.

She's tired. Not from the work itself—she loves the work. Strategy, negotiation, brand building—she was born for this. But the politics, the second-guessing, the layers of performance?

That's what drains her soul.

She once tried to talk about it—to hint at the pressure—with a senior colleague. A woman, even. The response?

"If you can't handle it, maybe this isn't for you."

It felt like a slap. Because this is exactly why she's here. To handle it. To change it. To prove that a young woman of color, with fire in her eyes and softness in her step, could lead—not despite who she is, but because of it.

It's 8:12 now. Anika breathes in, then out. She opens her planner—a battered Moleskine she carries everywhere. Tucked inside, a sticky note flutters. She wrote it months ago, on the day she almost quit:

"You don't have to be twice as good to be here. But you already are."

She smiles, just a little.

Not the performative kind she wears in the elevator. A real smile. The kind that says, I see you. I believe in you.

She smooths her blazer, picks up her bag, and walks out of the restroom like a warrior walking into battle—not loud, not armored—but steady. Ready.

Because she may not be the loudest voice in the room. But her presence? It's a power they haven't figured out how to measure yet.

he walks into the meeting room, breath steady but shallow, like she's holding herself in. Her heels click softly against the marble floor, each step echoing louder than the last. A hush of conversations, papers shuffling, laptops being plugged in—corporate ritual at its finest.

Mr. Rajan doesn't look up when she enters. Neither do the two senior managers who joined last quarter. She's early, but still invisible.

She takes a seat at the far end of the table. The "junior" end. The one where decisions don't get made, where you're seen but not necessarily heard. Her laptop hums as it wakes up, and so does she—rehearsing her pitch under her breath like a mantra. She's got numbers. She's got strategy. She's got receipts. But what she doesn't have is the luxury of just "winging it" the way her male colleagues do, laughing off errors with a casual shrug.

When the room fills, Mr. Rajan begins. No introductions. No acknowledgments. Just straight to business. Anika waits, watching the way ideas flow like a current—fast, aggressive, bouncing between the men like a ping-pong game she was never invited to play.

She raises her hand. A pause. A glance. He nods, reluctantly.

Her voice is calm, steady. She lays out the revised pitch, tightening the narrative, improving margins, leveraging insights from last quarter's data. One of the execs leans in. Another scribbles something down. Progress.

But then, just as she's gaining momentum, it happens. A man in a gray blazer—Rahul—cuts in. Repeats what she just said. Louder. Adds a dramatic "in essence, what I think she's trying to say is..." And suddenly, all heads turn to him.

Applause. Affirmation. Approval.

Her words, his voice.

She swallows the lump forming in her throat. She's not new to this. She knows what it feels like to be echoed without credit. To have your ideas stolen in real-time. To be a ghostwriter in your own success story.

But something in her cracks—quietly.

Not the kind of crack that breaks. The kind that opens.

Later that afternoon, in a glass-walled corner of the office, she's alone. Everyone's gone out for team lunch. She stayed back—told them she had calls. She didn't.

She opens her journal.

"I am done making myself small."

She writes it in capital letters. Underlines it twice.

Because this isn't just about a stolen idea or a missed promotion. It's about years of being told to adjust. Years of fitting herself into spaces that shrink her. Years of translating her power into something more "palatable."

She flips back through the journal—pages of frustration, quiet victories, lists of things she wanted to say but didn't.

Then she opens her laptop.

Subject line: Feedback + Next Steps

Body: A concise summary of the idea she pitched, the metrics she used, the projected outcomes, the timeline. She CCs Rahul. She CCs Mr. Rajan. She signs off:

"Looking forward to driving this forward, as discussed in today's meeting."

No exclamation points. No softeners. No "just checking in" or "hope this is okay." Just facts. Ownership. Fire.

She hits send.

The thrill isn't instant. It's slow-burning. A gentle kind of defiance. But she feels it—that shift. Like she's reclaiming something she didn't even realize she'd surrendered.

That night, she doesn't open her laptop. She doesn't recheck her email or review her analytics deck for the fiftieth time. She sits on her balcony, bare-faced, feet up, jasmine tea in hand. She watches the city lights blink like distant applause, and for the first time in weeks, she breathes like she means it.

The next morning, something shifts.

Rajan forwards her email to the leadership group. Adds a line:

"Great initiative from Anika. Let's align on this."

She doesn't smile. She doesn't thank him. Not yet.

Instead, she starts blocking out time on her calendar—an hour each week for strategy, an hour for mentorship, a thirty-minute slot titled "Self Check-In."

She begins speaking up earlier in meetings, not waiting for permission to take the floor. She shares her wins on LinkedIn—no apologies, no disclaimers. Just presence. Just truth.

And little by little, the office starts to adjust to her. Not the other way around.

She's still interrupted, still underestimated, still battling the slow-burn weight of bias—but now, she's not shrinking. She's showing up, with her full self.

A heroine. Not in a cape. In a blazer.

Not charging into war—but walking into work with her head high, her back straight, and a voice that will no longer be edited out of her own narrative.

Because in a world that tells women to be quiet achievers, Anika has decided to be something far more dangerous:

Visible.

Somewhere between the spreadsheets and the slammed doors, Anika stops flinching.

The shift isn't theatrical—it's subtle, deliberate. Like the earth tilting a fraction to catch the sun just right. She doesn't burst into rooms with a battle cry. She enters, calm as dawn, but with a gaze that says I see everything now.

The workplace doesn't change overnight, but she's no longer waiting for it to. She's learned that no promotion, no email forward, no office shoutout is a substitute for self-respect. Her worth is not up for review. Not quarterly. Not ever.

She begins mentoring interns—especially the ones who remind her of herself two years ago. Soft-spoken. Sharp-eyed. Afraid to take up space. She teaches them things no orientation ever will.

She says, "Take notes, but also take credit."

She says, "Don't dilute your ideas just to be digestible."

She says, "You belong—even when it feels like you don't."

They listen, wide-eyed. Because no one has told them this before.

The senior managers notice the shift. Some resent it. Some respect it. Some pretend not to see it at all. But she's not performing for them. Not anymore.

At home, the questions still come—"Are you eating properly? When are you taking a break? When are you getting married?"

She answers with a smile and changes the subject. She's done explaining that ambition isn't arrogance. That fulfillment doesn't come in one flavor. That her timeline doesn't need to be synchronized with anyone else's.

On weekends, she dances. Not in a class. Not for exercise. Just in her living room, barefoot, music blaring. She remembers what freedom feels like in her body. She takes herself out for breakfast dates. Orders exactly what she wants. Sits by the window and watches strangers go by, wondering how many women in this city are carrying the same invisible armor she wears.

One Thursday, she gets invited to speak at a women-in-leadership panel. The theme is Breaking the Glass Ceiling. She almost declines.

But then she thinks of every time she stayed silent in a room that didn't deserve her silence. Every time she thought maybe it's just me. Every sticky note she's ever written to keep herself from unraveling.

She says yes.

The night before the panel, she doesn't rehearse a speech. She doesn't look up statistics or quotes or talking points. Instead, she writes a letter. To herself. To the girl who cried in the bathroom stall at 8:13 a.m. To the girl who once wondered if confidence was something you had to fake forever. To the girl who thought being strong meant being quiet.

And the next morning, in a packed auditorium full of young professionals, she reads it out loud.

Her voice shakes a little at first. But it doesn't break.

When she finishes, the room is still. A beat of silence, then applause—not polite, but raw. Real. A woman in the front row wipes her eyes. Another stands up to clap first.

Afterwards, people come up to her—not just women. Men too. Saying thank you. Saying "me too." Saying, "You just put words to something I didn't know I was carrying."

And Anika realizes:
She didn't just break the glass ceiling. She picked up the shards, turned them into mirrors, and handed them to every woman who needed to see herself clearly again.

The office is still a battlefield. But now, she's not just surviving it. She's redesigning it.

One pitch.
One email.
One sticky note at a time.

And somewhere out there, another girl will walk into her first job and find a seat at the table that Anika carved out with quiet rage and relentless grace.

She'll sit down. Speak up. And think: I earned this.

Because now, she will know:

She's not an imposter.

She's not alone.

She's the heroine.

That evening, Anika walks out of the office building as the sky blushes into twilight. The glass facade reflects the fading sun and for once, she sees herself in it—not a shadow of someone else's expectations, but her own silhouette, standing tall, fierce, and absolutely unmissable.

She doesn't rush home. Instead, she stops at the tiny chai stand across the street. The one with the chipped mugs and the old radio playing Bollywood classics. The vendor knows her now. He nods, pours her a cup without asking.

She sips slowly, watching the city buzz past. Her phone lights up with another email—this time from HR.

"Would you be interested in leading a wellness initiative across the company? We want more women like you in the conversation."

She smiles.

She doesn't need a formal title to lead, but if they're finally asking the right questions—she'll answer. Loudly. Clearly. Authentically.

Because leadership isn't just about seats at tables or names on email chains. It's about legacy. About leaving doors open, not closed. About making sure the next girl walking in doesn't have to start from zero. About making space where none existed before and saying: Come in. Sit down. Speak up. You're not an outsider—you are the future.

And in that moment—sipping chai, her inbox buzzing, the city alive around her—Anika doesn't feel like a warrior or a rebel or a case study in diversity.

She just feels like herself.

Free.
Grounded.
Seen.

She throws the paper cup away, rolls up her sleeves, and heads back into the evening with that quiet, stormy fire in her chest.

The kind you don't notice right away.
But when it passes through,
it changes everything.

X

The Office Heroine - Reflection

What lies between the lines of Anika's story

Anika's journey speaks for a generation of women who've been told to be humble, grateful, small. But hidden within her narrative are lessons for any woman trying to navigate a space that wasn't built with her in mind.

Let's draw them out. Loud and proud.

Imposter Syndrome

A psychological pattern where a person doubts their accomplishments and has a persistent internalized fear of being exposed as a "fraud," despite evident success. It's not humility. It's the weight of systemic exclusion disguised as self-doubt.

It shows up quietly—when you hesitate before hitting "send," when you practice your introduction a dozen times, when you win something but feel like maybe... you just got lucky.

But here's the truth:
You didn't trick anyone. You worked for this. You earned this.

And that whisper inside your head that says "maybe I'm not good enough"?
That's not your voice.
That's centuries of gatekeeping. Internalized. Whispered back at you.

Anika's constant second-guessing isn't a personal flaw. It's a symptom of walking into spaces not built for her. When the default leader is still often a man, a certain body type, a certain tone of voice, then anyone who looks or speaks differently will feel like an outsider—even if they're overqualified. Imposter syndrome thrives in environments where praise is selective, mentorship is rare, and women are measured twice as harshly. Anika doesn't overcome it by "believing in herself more"—she overcomes it by slowly shifting the culture, refusing to internalize the silence anymore.

It's not always harassment or overt discrimination. Sometimes it's your ideas being rephrased by someone else and suddenly becoming "valuable." Sometimes it's being called "pushy" for doing what your male peers get promoted for. Sometimes it's the lack of eye contact in meetings, the "we didn't think of you for this role" with no real explanation, the surprise when you speak with authority.

What Anika experiences is death by a thousand small dismissals. And that's harder to name, harder to call out—but just as damaging.

When Anika sits in meetings as the only woman—or the only young woman of color—she carries more than just her project brief. She carries the pressure of representing all women, of disproving stereotypes just by breathing. This invisible labor is exhausting. She is expected to be assertive, but warm. Smart, but not intimidating. Strong, but emotionally intelligent. It's a tightrope walk, and every step feels like a test.

Anika's burnout isn't just from the workload. It's from the emotional tax of staying polite while being overlooked. Of navigating microaggressions with a smile. Of feeling like she has to overprepare to be taken seriously. Corporate spaces often celebrate "grit" while ignoring the erosion it causes inside. Mental health conversations still rarely touch on how much of women's stress is rooted in being unheard.

Notice how Anika doesn't just rise—she reaches back. This is how women climb systems that weren't built for them: not alone, but together. Through shared language, mutual validation, and unspoken codes of power. When Anika tells her interns to take credit, she's giving them something it took her years to learn. Mentorship isn't about hand-holding—it's about decoding the game, handing each other armor, and whispering "don't flinch."

When Anika takes that hour to dance. When she journals instead of overworking. When she blocks time on her calendar for herself—that is rebellion. That is resistance. In a world that profits off women's self-doubt and burnout, choosing to rest is not laziness—it's survival. And it's political.

For every reader who's ever questioned if they deserve their place at the table.

Anika's story is not unique—and that's what makes it so powerful. Because every city has a thousand Anikas. Women who show up, do the work, and still feel like they need to shrink to survive. Women who apologize for their brilliance. Who rehearse their sentences a dozen times before daring to raise a hand. Who get called "too emotional" when they speak up, and "too quiet" when they don't.

Her journey reminds us: success doesn't mean the struggle disappears. It means you get better at recognizing which battles are worth fighting—and how to fight them without losing yourself.

You don't have to burn out to prove your worth.
You don't need to perform perfection to belong.
You can be whole, and tired, and still powerful.

Visibility isn't a privilege. It's your birthright.

Dear Woman Who Deserves More,

If you're reading this, chances are you've felt it—the knot in your stomach when you speak up, the way your voice shakes even when your data is solid. You've sat in meetings with your hands under the table, clutching your fingers just to keep them from trembling. You've nodded along when people reworded your ideas and took credit. You've stared at your inbox, rereading your emails, wondering if you sounded too blunt... or too soft.

I see you. I was you.

Here's what I wish someone had told me earlier:

You don't have to be perfect to belong.

You don't have to be silent to be respected.

You don't have to be twice as good just to get half the credit—but you already are twice as good.

Your softness is not a liability. Your empathy is not weakness.

Your rage is not irrational. It is holy.

You will walk into rooms that aren't ready for you. Speak anyway.

You will be underestimated.

Let them. And then make them eat their doubts.

Some days, you'll want to give up. You'll question why you're trying so hard to be seen. But please—stay visible.

Because somewhere, another girl is watching you.
And your courage will give her permission to breathe a little deeper.

Don't wait for someone to hand you the mic. Build your own stage.

With you, always—
Anika

P.S. That thing you're afraid to say? Say it. Say it twice if they talk over you. Say it until they listen.

XI

Little Voices

Aarti woke up to the sound of honking cars, her mother's voice shouting orders to the younger siblings, and the shrill cry of a baby somewhere in the distance. The sun was barely up, but already, the streets outside her small, cramped home were alive with the frantic pulse of the city. It was a noise she'd grown used to, the kind of noise that seeped into your bones and settled there, thick and unrelenting. But today, as she lay under the thin blanket that didn't quite keep the cold out, the noise felt louder, as if it was trying to drown her.

She wanted to stay under the covers. She wanted to pull the world away and disappear, to hide from the gnawing ache that had been with her for so long. But that wasn't an option. There were mouths to feed, younger siblings to take care of, and a mother who relied on her to help at the roadside stall. So, Aarti pulled herself up, as she always did, and fought the heaviness that seemed to weigh down her every movement. The floorboards creaked under her feet, echoing in the small room like a warning.

She could hear the murmur of her mother's voice outside, urging the younger ones to start getting ready for school. Aarti glanced at the modest pile of clothes she had worn the day before—dirty, but clean enough to wear again. She didn't mind. She had long stopped caring about appearances. What did it matter when the world only saw you as the girl who helped her mother with the shop? What did it matter when survival was the only thing on the menu for the day?

Her eyes drifted toward the small mirror on the wall. She didn't recognize the girl staring back at her. She was thin, with dark circles under her eyes, her skin pale in the harsh light that streamed through the tiny window. Her hair, once long and shiny, now hung in dull, lifeless strands around her face. She was 16, but in that moment, she felt much older.

The reflection didn't seem to belong to her. It was like looking at a stranger.

She turned away quickly, unwilling to linger on the person she had become. It had been like this for months, maybe longer—this feeling of being trapped inside her own body, as if she were watching her life from the outside. There was a part of her that wanted to scream, to throw herself onto the floor and demand that someone listen. But there was no one to hear her.

And that was the worst part.

No one had ever taught her how to speak about what she felt. No one had ever told her that it was okay to be sad, to feel weak, to need help. In her world, emotions were a luxury. The kind of thing that rich people had the time and space to deal with. For people like her, there was only the constant grind—wake up, work, survive. Emotions were something that took up space, and space was something they didn't have.

Aarti pushed the thought out of her mind and forced herself into action. She dressed quickly in the worn clothes that would have to do. Her mother was already bustling around the kitchen, preparing tea and calling out instructions to the younger children, who were still half asleep. It was a routine that had been drilled into her since she was old enough to walk. Every morning, every day, was the same.

She barely said a word as she shuffled over to the small stall outside, where her mother sold vegetables, fruits, and a few other odds and ends. The busy street was alive with the clatter of vendors shouting their wares, the screech of rickshaws, and the occasional honk of a car speeding by. It was all too much. The sounds felt like they were pounding against her skull, louder than the beat of her own heart.

But she kept going, because that's what you did. You kept going.

Aarti was good at pretending. She had to be. She had learned early on that if you didn't smile, if you didn't nod your head when someone spoke to you, if you didn't do what was expected of you, then you would be forgotten. People didn't have time to care about you when they had their own problems to deal with. Her mother, though kind, was too busy trying to make ends meet to notice the tiredness in Aarti's eyes, or the way she flinched when a stranger spoke to her.

No one noticed.

And if they did, they didn't know what to do with it.

As the day dragged on, Aarti found herself slipping deeper into the haze that had become her life. Her head ached, her stomach twisted in knots, but she kept working, kept moving.

By noon, the crowd had thinned. Most of the vendors packed up their stalls, leaving Aarti and her mother alone with their little corner of the market. Aarti took a seat on a crate behind the stall and closed her eyes, hoping for just a moment of silence. But the world wouldn't give her that. The noise continued to rage around her, louder than ever. The weight on her chest felt heavier, suffocating.

"Aarti, are you okay?"

Her mother's voice startled her. She opened her eyes and looked up at her mother, who stood in front of her, eyes soft with concern. Aarti hesitated. She wanted to tell her everything—the sadness that had been gnawing at her insides for so long, the feeling that she was disappearing. But the words got stuck in her throat.

"I'm fine," Aarti muttered, forcing a smile she didn't feel. Her mother gave her a dubious look, but nodded and turned back to the stall. Aarti's heart sank.

She wasn't fine.

She hadn't been fine for a long time.

In the silence that followed, Aarti's thoughts swirled. What was wrong with her? Why couldn't she just be happy like everyone else? Why did the weight of the world feel like it was crushing her every second of the day? She remembered the old adage her mother often repeated: "Don't let your emotions control you. You have to be strong, for the family."

But what if she couldn't be strong anymore?

A tiny voice in her head whispered the words she'd never dared to say out loud: "I'm not okay."

The sound of the street, the chatter of people going by, the calls of the vendors—all of it seemed to fade away for a moment. The voice was small, almost too faint to hear. But for the first time in so long, it felt like the weight was being lifted, just a little. The silence that followed felt like a moment of clarity, a fleeting glimpse of something Aarti had never known—permission to feel, to break, to not be okay.

But that moment didn't last long. The noise of the world crept back in, and Aarti was left alone with her thoughts. She didn't know what to do with the small voice inside her, the voice that whispered of sadness, of yearning, of needing something more.

She didn't know how to make it louder, or who would listen if she did.

But she knew one thing for sure: It couldn't stay quiet forever.

The rest of the afternoon passed in a blur. Aarti moved through the motions—arranging the fruits and vegetables, packing them into bags, and offering polite smiles to the few customers who passed by. But her mind was elsewhere, lost in a storm of thoughts that refused to settle. The voice inside her, the one that whispered "I'm not okay", kept growing louder, echoing in the space where there was no room for it.

She tried to drown it out. She tried to keep busy, to focus on anything other than what was happening inside her. But it was impossible. It felt like the weight of the world was pressing down on her chest, and no matter how much she tried to breathe, the air felt thin, suffocating.

By the time the sun began to set, casting long shadows over the street, Aarti could feel the exhaustion creeping into her bones. Her eyes were heavy, her limbs like lead, and she longed for the relief of sleep that didn't come. When her mother announced it was time to head home, Aarti moved slowly, too tired to protest.

That night, as she lay in her small, makeshift bed, the silence of the room felt almost unbearable. Her mother was already asleep, the soft rhythm of her breathing filling the quiet. Aarti stared up at the ceiling, her mind racing with thoughts she couldn't quiet.

What was wrong with her? Why did she feel so empty, so broken? Why couldn't she just be like everyone else—strong, resilient, able to push through the hardships of life without falling apart?

Her eyes wandered to the corner of the room where a small bundle of books sat. Among the pile was a crumpled piece of paper—one of the pamphlets from the local clinic that she had spotted earlier in the day. The bright colors and bold letters caught her attention, and for a brief moment, a flicker of curiosity stirred in her. She had picked it up without thinking, folding it neatly and shoving it into her bag when no one was looking.

Now, she reached over and pulled the pamphlet out, her fingers trembling slightly as she unfolded it. The words on the page were simple, but they hit her like a wave:

"Mental health is just as important as physical health. You are not alone. There is help available. Reach out. Speak up."

Aarti stared at the words for a long time, her heart pounding in her chest. Was it possible? Was there really help out there for her? Was she allowed to feel what she was feeling, to admit that something was wrong?

The thought was both terrifying and liberating.

The next morning, as the first rays of sunlight filtered through the window, Aarti felt a shift inside her. It was small, like a crack in the wall she had built around herself. The pamphlet still sat on her bedside table, its words lingering in her mind. She didn't know what it meant, or what kind of help it promised, but the fact that someone had written those words—that someone cared enough to make that pamphlet—gave her a tiny sliver of hope.

She didn't know what to do with that hope, but she knew she couldn't ignore it anymore.

The day dragged on in the same routine—selling at the stall, watching the world spin around her as she went through the motions. But even in the midst of the chaos, she couldn't stop thinking about the pamphlet. What if she went to the clinic? What if she spoke to someone about how she felt?

The thought made her stomach twist, but it also made her heart beat faster. For the first time in months, Aarti felt a flicker of something other than emptiness. It wasn't much, but it was enough to spark the smallest flame of possibility.

That evening, after the last customer had left the stall and her mother was tidying up, Aarti slipped away. She told her mother she was going to the market to buy something. It wasn't a lie—she just didn't know how to say the truth.

She walked through the streets, the noise still deafening, but it felt different now, like she was walking through it with a purpose. She reached the clinic a little while later, its faded sign barely visible in the dim light. Taking a deep breath, Aarti pushed open the door.

The clinic was small, with peeling paint and a faint smell of antiseptic in the air. But it felt safe, in a way. The receptionist looked up from her desk, her face soft with curiosity.

"How can I help you?" she asked.

Aarti froze. Her mouth went dry. She opened her mouth to speak but nothing came out. She felt the familiar rush of panic rise up in her chest, but this time, something was different. She wasn't going to turn away. She wasn't going to hide.

"I... I need to talk to someone," she managed to say, her voice barely above a whisper.

The receptionist's eyes softened. She nodded and gestured to a door in the back. "Come in. We'll see what we can do."

As Aarti stepped into the small, quiet room, she felt the weight of the world pressing down on her, but she also felt something else—a sense of relief. She didn't know what was going to happen next, but she knew she had taken the first step. She had spoken up. She had reached out.

And for the first time in a long while, she felt like she wasn't invisible anymore.

The counselor, a woman with kind eyes and a calm voice, invited Aarti to sit. There was no judgment in her gaze, no rushing to tell Aarti what she should feel or how she should act. Just the space to be, to exist in her brokenness, without having to pretend.

Aarti took a deep breath. This was it—the beginning of something new.

"I don't know what's wrong with me," she said quietly, her voice shaking. "I feel... so empty. All the time."

The counselor nodded, her voice gentle. "That's okay. You don't have to have all the answers right now. We'll figure this out together."

For the first time, Aarti allowed herself to believe that someone, somewhere, might just understand.

The session felt like a strange kind of release for Aarti, as if she were finally exhaling after holding her breath for far too long. She wasn't used to talking about herself, especially not the things she had buried so deep inside. But with every word she spoke, every feeling she let out into the room, the weight on her chest seemed to ease just a little bit.

The counselor's voice was calm, soothing, like a lifeline in a stormy sea. She didn't rush Aarti, didn't push her to speak more than she was ready to. She simply listened. And for the first time in Aarti's life, someone made her feel like her pain was real, like it mattered.

"I've never said these things out loud before," Aarti admitted, her voice barely above a whisper. "I've never even told my mom... or anyone. I don't know what's wrong with me, why I feel this way."

The counselor nodded again, her expression soft but understanding. "You're not alone in feeling like this, Aarti. It's okay to feel lost sometimes. And it's okay to need help. You've taken a huge step by coming here today."

Aarti felt a lump form in her throat. She wanted to believe the counselor's words, but there was a part of her that still felt like she was making too big a deal out of it. Her family, her community—no one had the luxury of worrying about things like sadness when there were so many other problems to solve. The voices in her head still whispered that she wasn't allowed to feel this way, that there were more important things to focus on than her emotions.

But the counselor's steady presence kept her grounded, and little by little, the walls she had built around herself began to crumble. The conversation wasn't magic; it didn't make everything better right away. But it was a start.

"Why do you think you feel this way, Aarti?" the counselor asked, leaning forward slightly, her eyes kind and patient.

Aarti bit her lip. She hadn't really thought about it in those terms. What made her feel this way? Was it the poverty, the constant struggle? Was it the unspoken weight of expectations, the way her entire life had been built on survival and endurance? Or was it something more subtle, more internal—an emotion she had never learned to name?

"I don't know," she admitted, feeling vulnerable. "It's everything, I guess. It's like... I'm always tired. Not just physically. Inside, too. And I don't know how to talk about it. I feel like if I do, people will say it's just stress, or that I should be stronger. But it's more than that. I feel... empty, I guess."

The counselor was quiet for a moment, nodding in understanding. "It sounds like you've been carrying a heavy burden, Aarti. And carrying it alone is exhausting. But you don't have to do it alone anymore. There are people who want to help, who can help you carry it. You don't have to keep silent about your pain."

Aarti swallowed hard, feeling a strange mix of relief and fear. Relief that someone else saw her pain, that it wasn't just in her head. But fear, too—fear of what it meant to truly let go, to speak her truth and not hide behind the mask she had worn for so long.

For the rest of the session, they talked more—about her life, her family, the things that made her happy, the things that made her sad. It was exhausting and cathartic in ways Aarti hadn't expected. But when she left the clinic, she felt different. Not fixed, not healed—but lighter, somehow, as if she had taken a small but meaningful step toward something better.

As she walked back through the bustling streets, the sounds of the city felt less deafening, less oppressive. She still heard the honking of the cars, the chatter of vendors, the cries of children playing. But now, the noise didn't seem to swallow her whole. It was just background noise to the quiet, steady rhythm of her own thoughts.

She didn't know exactly where this path would lead. The idea of seeking help still felt foreign to her, something outside the realm of what she had been taught. But the pamphlet she had found, the words that had echoed in her mind, now felt like a promise—a promise that there was a way forward, even if she couldn't see the entire road yet.

The next morning, Aarti woke up to the same cacophony of noise, the same demands of daily life. But something was different. She felt less overwhelmed, less alone in her own head. As she helped her mother at the stall, she found herself smiling more, her interactions with the customers more genuine. Her thoughts were still a whirlwind, but for the first time in a long time, she felt like she had the strength to face them.

That evening, after a long day, Aarti found herself sitting quietly at the small table in their cramped home, watching the sun set outside. Her mother was busy preparing dinner, her younger siblings playing in the corner. Aarti felt a sudden pang of longing—longing for a life where she didn't have to carry so much, where she didn't have to be the strong one all the time. But at the same time, she felt something else—a glimmer of hope, a possibility that she hadn't felt before.

She hadn't talked to her mother about what happened at the clinic yet. The thought of it made her stomach tighten. But she knew she would, eventually. She knew that the hardest part was over—that she had taken the first step toward change, and that the silence didn't have to define her anymore.

The voice inside her, the one that had whispered "I'm not okay", was still there. But now, it wasn't a secret anymore. It was a voice she could share, a voice that mattered.

And that was enough—for now.

She kept going to the clinic, every week, even though it felt like an awkward foreign routine at first. But the more she spoke with the counselor, the more she realized that she didn't have to carry everything in silence. She didn't have to hide her pain or shame. She didn't have to make herself smaller to fit into a world that didn't leave space for vulnerability.

Each conversation felt like an unraveling, a slow process of shedding the skin of the person she used to be. The girl who buried her emotions, who was so used to pretending everything was okay. With every word she spoke, Aarti realized that the silence she had lived with for so long wasn't her fault. It wasn't her burden to carry alone.

But no one in her community seemed to understand. There were no open conversations about mental health, no discussions about how to handle stress, how to deal with the weight of a life that was always about survival. People didn't talk about being tired of fighting. People didn't talk about needing help, because needing help was seen as weakness. It was one of the many unspoken rules of the community.

That knowledge was always in the back of Aarti's mind, tugging at her with the quiet pressure of guilt. Her mother, her siblings—they would never understand what was happening inside her. They didn't have the luxury of sitting in a room with a counselor and processing their emotions. They had to work, to survive. There was no time for self-care, no space for soft words of comfort. It was survival of the fittest, plain and simple.

But as Aarti spent more time at the clinic, as she slowly allowed herself to become someone who could talk about how she felt, she started to notice something shifting within herself. There was a part of her, buried deep beneath the weight of her life, that still wanted to fight for something more. She wanted more than just getting by. She wanted a life where she could feel seen, where she could feel heard. She wanted a life where she could take up space, where she didn't have to apologize for existing.

One afternoon, after her session at the clinic, Aarti found herself walking back to the stall with a new kind of determination. She was tired, yes—bone-deep tired—but her mind felt clearer than it had in a long time. She still didn't have all the answers, but for the first time, she felt like she didn't need them all at once. She was learning to be okay with not knowing everything, with not having it all figured out.

As she approached the market, the familiar sounds hit her—shouts from the vendors, the clatter of metal, the hum of the busy street. But it didn't overwhelm her the way it used to. She didn't feel like she was being swallowed up by it anymore. She was part of it, but it didn't define her.

Her mother was already at the stall, arranging the produce with practiced hands. Aarti paused for a moment, watching her mother's movements. The woman was strong, a force of nature, always putting others first. Aarti had spent years trying to live up to that strength, trying to be just like her. But now, she understood something she hadn't before: strength didn't mean never being vulnerable. It didn't mean keeping everything inside and pretending to be invincible.

Strength was allowing yourself to ask for help when you needed it.

"Ma," Aarti said, her voice quieter than usual. She wasn't sure how to start the conversation, how to bridge the gap between the silent daughter and the mother who never showed her own pain.

Her mother looked up, raising an eyebrow. "What is it, beta?"

Aarti hesitated. She had never been able to speak openly with her mother about her feelings. The weight of years of silence made the words feel heavy, clumsy, almost foreign. But the pamphlet from the clinic, the counselor's gentle encouragement, the small breakthrough she had felt in that quiet room—it all pressed her forward.

"I... I've been feeling... a little lost, Ma," Aarti said, her words stumbling out. She could feel her heart race as the words left her mouth. I've been feeling lost. It wasn't something that could be easily brushed off. But it was the truth, and for the first time, Aarti felt the weight of it lift off her chest.

Her mother's face softened, but there was a trace of confusion in her eyes. "Lost?" she asked, her voice cautious. "But you're fine, no? You work hard, you help here... you're always doing something."

Aarti shook her head. "I don't think you understand, Ma. It's not about working. I feel... empty sometimes. Like I'm just going through the motions, but I don't feel like I'm really here. And it's getting harder to ignore."

Her mother paused, her hands stilling over a bundle of vegetables. Aarti watched her, waiting for the response that would determine if this was a conversation that could go any further.

The silence between them stretched long, thick with unspoken words. Then, finally, her mother sighed, her expression shifting as if she were seeing Aarti for the first time.

"I don't know how to fix it, beta," she said quietly, her voice thick with emotion. "I don't know how to make you feel better. All I know is that we have to keep going, that we have to keep working. But if... if you need something more than that, I'll try. I'll try to understand."

Aarti felt a lump form in her throat. It wasn't the kind of response she had expected, but it was enough. Her mother didn't have the answers, but she was willing to listen. And that was more than Aarti had ever dared hope for.

"I'm seeing someone," Aarti said, her voice small but steady. "A counselor. She helps me talk about how I'm feeling. It's... it's helping. I think I just need to keep going."

Her mother's eyes softened even more, and Aarti saw something flicker in her—a mix of relief and sadness. "I don't know what that is, but if it helps you, I'm glad," her mother said. "I want you to be happy, beta. I just don't always know how to help."

And for the first time in her life, Aarti realized that her mother wasn't perfect. She wasn't the unshakable pillar of strength that Aarti had always imagined. She, too, was human, just like her. And that was okay. Maybe, just maybe, they didn't have to carry everything alone.

As the evening wore on and the sun dipped below the horizon, Aarti felt a strange peace settle over her. It wasn't an answer, but it was progress. She was learning to speak her truth, to claim her voice, even in a world that tried to silence it. She was learning that she didn't have to hide her pain, that she didn't have to disappear in order to survive.

And as she watched her mother go about preparing dinner, she felt a new kind of hope—small, fragile, but real. It was a hope that maybe, just maybe, things didn't have to be this hard forever.

Maybe, someday, she could find a way to feel whole again.

The weeks that followed weren't perfect. There were days when Aarti felt overwhelmed, when the weight of everything seemed too much to bear. But they were fewer now. Each day, she woke up and made a choice—not to be okay, not to be perfect, but to keep going. To keep reaching for the space where she could breathe, where she could just be.

The sessions at the clinic continued, each one slowly but surely chiseling away at the walls she had built around herself. She spoke about her fears, her dreams, and her disappointments. It wasn't easy, but with every word, the emptiness inside her seemed to fill up, not with answers, but with understanding—understanding that her emotions didn't have to be a source of shame, that feeling lost didn't mean she was weak.

One evening, as she sat in the small courtyard outside her home, Aarti looked up at the sky, her eyes tracing the stars that flickered like tiny promises. The city was loud as always, but there was a quiet peace inside her now, a peace she had never known.

Her mother came out to join her, sitting next to her in the cool evening air. For a while, neither of them spoke. Aarti didn't feel the need to fill the silence. It wasn't uncomfortable anymore. It was just two people—two women—sitting together in the stillness, sharing a moment without words.

Finally, her mother broke the silence. "I'm proud of you, beta," she said softly. "For going to the clinic. For taking care of yourself. I know it's not easy, but I'm proud."

Aarti turned to her, surprised by the sincerity in her mother's voice. She had expected to hear the usual words of strength, the ones that pushed her to keep going without stopping. But this was different. This was the acknowledgment that sometimes, the hardest thing was simply to ask for help.

"I'm proud of you too, Ma," Aarti whispered, her voice thick with emotion. "I think... I think we're both learning."

Her mother nodded, a soft smile tugging at her lips. "Yes. We are."

And in that moment, Aarti realized something—something simple but profound. Healing wasn't a straight line. It wasn't something you could rush or force. It was a journey, a slow unfolding of understanding, of strength, of vulnerability. And it wasn't something she had to do alone.

As she looked up at the stars again, she felt something shift within her. It was a feeling of quiet determination, of hope not born from certainty, but from the belief that maybe, just maybe, she was allowed to take up space in this world—allowed to feel, allowed to break, allowed to rebuild.

And that was enough.

Aarti closed her eyes, letting the night settle around her. She wasn't fixed. She wasn't perfect. But she was real. And for the first time in a long time, that was more than enough.

She wasn't invisible anymore.

And that was the beginning.

XII

Little Voices - Reflection

Mental health is often one of the most overlooked aspects of well-being in low-income communities, where the focus is often on survival rather than self-care. In Aarti's story, her battle with depression is not just about the personal struggles she faces but also about the systemic issues that prevent individuals like her from accessing the help they need.

A key problem in many low-income areas is the lack of access to mental health resources. Counseling services, therapy, and mental health education are often seen as luxuries—services that those struggling to make ends meet cannot afford or even consider. In communities where day-to-day survival is the top priority, mental health is often an afterthought. And for someone like Aarti, who lives in a community where emotions are often suppressed and weakness is stigmatized, asking for help is not just difficult—it feels impossible. The deep-rooted silence around mental health struggles exacerbates feelings of isolation, making it harder for people to speak out and find support.

Moreover, mental health is often misunderstood. It's not seen as a valid issue that requires professional help but instead as something to "get over" or "push through." This mindset is reinforced by cultural expectations to be strong and resilient, especially in families where every member is expected to contribute to the collective effort of survival. This perpetuates a dangerous cycle of untreated mental health issues, where people suffer in silence, often for years.

The need for mental health resources in these communities is urgent. Schools, clinics, and local organizations should not only provide basic healthcare but also integrate mental health services as part of the overall care package. Additionally, raising awareness about mental health in these communities, breaking the stigma, and providing affordable, accessible services are essential steps in ensuring that individuals like Aarti don't have to face their struggles alone.

As Aarti's journey continues, it's clear that the road to healing is neither short nor easy. But her story speaks to something bigger than just her personal experience—it's a call for change. Aarti's ability to speak up, to seek help, and to navigate the barriers of silence and stigma is not just a personal victory. It's a reflection of the potential for growth and healing in communities where mental health is often neglected or misunderstood.

Aarti's journey is just one of many, but it represents a growing movement to break the silence surrounding mental health. It is a movement that says: It's okay to not be okay, and It's okay to ask for help. Healing starts when we acknowledge that our pain is valid, our struggles are real, and that we deserve care—both physical and emotional.

Dear One,

I see you. I know you're out there, fighting silently. You're the one who wakes up every day, carrying a weight that no one can see. You push through the exhaustion, the fear, the emptiness—and you do it all without anyone noticing, without anyone asking if you're okay.

I've been where you are. I know how it feels to believe that your emotions don't matter, that you have to keep going, no matter what. I know how it feels to bury everything inside because the world around you doesn't make space for vulnerability.

But listen—your pain matters. You don't have to be strong all the time. You don't have to pretend that everything is fine when it's not. It's okay to feel lost, to feel tired, to feel like you're not enough. And it's okay to ask for help. You don't have to carry it all alone.

I know that there are no easy answers, and there are days when everything feels overwhelming. But I promise you, there is a way out. It's not a quick fix, and it won't happen overnight. But the first step is speaking up. Find someone you trust. Talk about how you're feeling. Even if it's just one person, it's a start.

You are worthy of love, care, and support. Don't let anyone tell you otherwise. You don't have to keep quiet about your struggles. You are allowed to take up space. You are allowed to feel. And most importantly, you are allowed to heal.

I'm walking this path too, and I'm here, cheering you on. Keep going. There is light, even if you can't see it yet.

With love and hope,

Aarti

AFTERWORD

Each of the stories in The Silent Superwomen is fictional, but the emotions they reflect are very real. They were inspired by countless untold experiences—the silent struggles of women and girls who continue to show up for the world, often without anyone asking how they're truly doing.

Whether it was the quiet resilience of The Healer Who Hurts, the isolation behind The Masked Mother, or the emotional weight carried by The Office Heroine and The Teenage Warrior—every character in this collection was created to represent the complexity and depth of real women's inner lives.

If you saw yourself in these pages, or someone you know, I hope you walk away with a little more empathy, a little more courage to speak up, and a lot less guilt for needing rest, help, or healing.

To every silent superwoman reading this: You are allowed to pause. You are allowed to feel. And you are never alone.

GLOSSARY

Anxiety – A feeling of worry, nervousness, or unease, often about an upcoming event or something with an uncertain outcome. Chronic anxiety can interfere with daily life and is a common mental health condition.

Burnout – A state of emotional, physical, and mental exhaustion caused by prolonged stress, often from work or caregiving roles. It can lead to feelings of helplessness, detachment, and loss of motivation.

Caregiver Fatigue – Emotional and physical exhaustion experienced by those who provide long-term care for someone else, often leading to feelings of resentment, guilt, or isolation.

Emotional Labor – The process of managing one's emotions to meet the expectations of others, often in professional or personal roles. It's frequently invisible and expected from women.

Imposter Syndrome – The internal experience of believing that one's success is undeserved, often accompanied by self-doubt and fear of being exposed as a "fraud."

Mental Health – A person's emotional, psychological, and social well-being. It affects how we think, feel, and act, and it influences how we handle stress, relate to others, and make choices.

Perfectionism – A personality trait where a person strives for flawlessness and sets extremely high standards, often accompanied by critical self-evaluations and fear of failure.

Postpartum Depression (PPD) – A form of depression that occurs after childbirth, affecting the mother's mood, energy, and ability to care for herself or her baby. It's treatable and not a sign of weakness.

Silent Struggles – Emotional or mental battles a person goes through internally, often without expressing them outwardly or seeking help. These are at the heart of many stories in this book.

Stigma – A negative attitude or discrimination against someone based on a distinguishing characteristic, such as mental illness. Stigma often prevents people from seeking help.

Support System – The network of people (family, friends, therapists, peers) who offer emotional, psychological, or practical help during challenging times.

Therapy – A treatment process where a trained professional helps a person understand and manage their emotions, thoughts, and behaviors. Therapy can be individual, group-based, or family-centered.

Trauma – A deeply distressing or disturbing experience that can have long-lasting emotional effects. It can result from events like abuse, loss, accidents, or prolonged stress.

Resources & Support

If you or someone you know is struggling with mental health, here are some resources that offer support, information, and connection:

iCall (India): +91 9152987821 — Free mental health support

AASRA: +91 9820466726 — 24/7 helpline for emotional crisis

NIMHANS (India): nimhans.ac.in — Leading mental health research and care

The Live Love Laugh Foundation: thelivelovelaughfoundation.org

Snehi (Delhi): 91-11-65978181 — Counseling for youth and families

If you are outside India, please consult local mental health hotlines or organizations in your region.

9 7 9 8 8 9 9 0 6 6 8 8 7